Writing the Family Narrative
WORKBOOK

by Lawrence P. Gouldrup, Ph.D.

 ancestry publishing

Library of Congress Cataloging-in-Publication Data

Gouldrup, Lawrence P.
Writing the family narrative workbook / Lawrence P. Gouldrup
p.   cm.
Includes bibliographical references.

ISBN-13: 978-0-916489-41-0
ISBN-10: 0-916489-41-8

1. Genealogy—Authorship—Problems, exercises, etc.   2. Report writing—Problems, exercises, etc.   I. Title.
CS21 .G68   1993   808'.066929—dc20
95112353

Published by
Ancestry Publishing, a division of
The Generations Network, Inc.
360 West 4800 North
Provo, Utah 84604
www.ancestry.com

First printing 1993
10 9 8 7 6

CONTENTS

PREFACE

After reading *Writing the Family Narrative* (*WFN*), you may well have observed that you know now what has to be done but that you do not know how to do it. No matter how clear and obvious a discussion of writing principles might be, there is no substitute for being "walked" through the process of writing.

This workbook is a "walk" through the writing process and is first an extension of the principles and the examples presented in *WFN*, and more importantly, a practical guide to the writer who wants to apply those principles. You will recognize in this *Workbook* the principles presented in *WFN* and will be familiar with the illustrations which have been both extended and elaborated upon here. Each chapter in the *Workbook* corresponds to a chapter in *WFN*. You will note the correspondence in the titles of each chapter.

Each chapter in the *Workbook* also contains a number of exercises that will help you master the concepts of *WFN* and begin writing the family narrative. You may complete the exercises with reference to one specific portion of your family history, or you may complete them with reference to many different individuals, family lines, and eras. The exercises can be referred to again and again as an effective way to begin writing about any portion of your family history.

CHAPTER 1

ESTABLISHING DIRECTIONS

WHAT IS FAMILY HISTORY?

How should I tell my story? As amazing as it may seem, most people who set out to write a family history have no clear idea how to tell the story. They have read few if any family histories, much less even considered the possibility that reading is a prerequisite to the writing of a good family history. There are as many ways to tell one's story as there are storytellers, and writers in all walks of life, professional as well as amateur, have tried their hand at writing the family story. Some have written their stories deliberately, the writing of family history being their primary focus; others have written their family story almost as an afterthought, having made their mark as writers in other fields. James A. Michener, in his essay "The Book That Made a Difference," tells how when he read Thomas Mann's *Buddenbrooks* he "discovered how to construct a narrative that covers more than one generation, and then I had my armament for the long battles ahead." There are literally hundreds of useful and comfortable approaches that can be ours simply for the reading, and the way to answer the question "How should I tell my story?" is first to ask how others have told their stories.

The range and variety of writings in *WFN* chapter 1 that make up the definition "family literature" argue for a range and variety of approaches. In addition to these ideas, the following are approaches which a writer might also consider:

A Fitting Habitation by Agnes Rothery: the houses this couple occupied become the means of presenting the family history.

All Creatures Great and Small by James Herriot: the author's experiences treating animals become the vehicle for presenting the author's life story as well as the story of his relationship with his veterinarian coworkers and the countless people he encounters in Yorkshire.

Brothers Karamazov by Ivan Dostoevsky: a story of bad relations, murder, and family disruption framed as a novel.

Dear Dad by Louis Anderson: the author addresses a series of letters to his father in which he works out his trauma as an adult child of an alcoholic parent.

Genesis: a series of family stories based around the basic theme of sibling rivalry, familial disruption, and reconciliation.

In My Father's House: Tales of an Unconformable Man by Nancy Huddleston Packer: a series of seven stories related only in that they explore one man's personality and his impact on others.

John Ransom's Andersonville Diary by Bruce Catton: chapters break up the diary and join with addenda that provide important background material to the diary entries.

Legacy by James A. Michener: an eight-generation family novel built around the relationship of each generation to the constitution.

Letters from Bath, 1766-1767 by the Rev. John Penrose by Brigitte Mitchell and Hubert Penrose: the letters follow an introduction which describes the family members and the town and society of Bath.

Like Water for Chocolate by Laura Esquivel: a family novel in monthly installments with recipes, romances, and home remedies.

Marriott: the J. Willard Marriott Story by Robert O'Brien: a few introductory chapters on the family history lead into a biography of J. Willard Marriott.

Refuge: An Unnatural History of Family and Place by Terry Tempest Williams: the author employs natural history as the image through which she charts the progress of cancer through the female members of her family.

Seven Stories of Christmas Love by Leo Buscaglia: seven stories based on Christmas memories and arranged chronologically capture the author's life story.

The Little Land of Cornwall by A.L. Rowse: Rowse combines a collection of short biographies and family histories with descriptions of buildings, institutions, and landscapes to present Cornwall.

Winesburg, Ohio by Sherwood Anderson: biographies of local inhabitants weave into and combine with the main biography of a young reporter who finally leaves the small town to make his way in the world.

Wolf Willow by Wallace Stegner: a portrait of a pioneer Saskatchewan community based on the author's recollection of his boyhood days.

Exercise 1-1

Begin a list of approaches others have used in telling a story, ways that you particularly like and might be able to use in telling your story.

1. _____

_____

2. _____

_____

3. _____

_____

4. _____

_____

5. _____

_____

6. _____

_____

7. _____

_____

8. _____

_____

9. _____

_____

10. _____

_____

11. _____

_____

12. _____

_____

13. _____

_____

14. _____

_____

There is one other very important ingredient to telling your story: tell the truth. No one believes or wants an idealized portrait, it simply does not ring true. Susan Allen Troth in her warm portrait of her father, "Missing, A Man With A Briefcase," makes this very important point, referring finally to the time that her father washed her mouth out with soap:

> "Can you think of anything bad about my father?" I once asked my Uncle Don, his only brother. He and my aunt looked puzzled. There was an awkward pause. "It's just that he doesn't quite seem real," I tried to explain, but my words hung like discordant notes over the luncheon table, jarring them into silence. I knew then that I was asking questions no one could answer anymore.
>
> My father's idealized portrait has hung, lit with a loving glow, in his family's and friends' memories for forty-two years: a tall, almost handsome, eager man, who knew how to laugh, who sang and danced and played tennis, who worked hard and brilliantly at his career. I grew up with this portrait, and I am glad I have it. But I long for a few flaws to make it come alive. I sometimes wonder if that is why I remember so vividly the taste of soap in my mouth.

> — Carolyn Anthony, *Family Portraits*

Always remember that unless you balance the flaws with the ideal, your story will simply not "be alive" and you will not be believed.

CHAPTER 2

LAYING THE FACTUAL FOUNDATION

Using Records to Write the Historical Exposition

ORGANIZING GENEALOGICAL RECORDS

Most family historians start out as genealogists, and even if they do not, they probably should. Conceivably one could write the history of his immediate family without any recourse to the principles of genealogical research. But family history that reaches beyond the immediate family essentially must be based on the "family tree." The problem for the family historian is how to organize and control the mass of information that comprises the family record in such a way as to facilitate the writing process. Increasingly today, genealogists turn to computer programs to help them organize the names and dates that make up the usual genealogical record. There are many good programs on the market, but the one that I have used and found to be the most versatile is the LDS Genealogical Department's Personal Ancestral File program. All programs on the market today, however, are adequate to the essential task of giving the family historian a sense of control and focus. The chief value of these programs is that they organize genealogical or family history information into various levels of specificity or abstraction thus allowing the historian absolute freedom and complete ease in the writing of history. Consider my surname pedigrees and related family group chart on the following pages.

These various charts actually comprise three levels of specificity. Normally genealogists break all genealogical charts into two broad categories: the family group sheet and the pedigree chart. But it is far more helpful for the writer of family history to see these charts as forming three levels of specificity, the essential first step in the process of writing. See the illustrations on the following pages for an explanation of how different charts meet different writing needs.

The family group record or the individual record is the logical place to begin. The individual record becomes the biography, the family group record the family history. However, successful writing depends directly on the detail available, and neither of these most specific of forms contains sufficient detail. The best approach is to use these computer printouts as indexes to hard-copy files that contain the detail. The normal individual record or family group sheet each has a note field, but it is probably better to have the note sections refer briefly or generally to items of which the files contain detailed documents or excerpts. The brief summaries in the note sections of each of these computer forms refer to detailed hard-copy files.

Obviously, these forms dictate the kind of history we will write: they force us to see history as the record of individuals or as individuals organized into families. If the writer chooses to be more abstract, the pedigree overview and the pedigree chart, however, do permit the historian to see history as family lines. Conceivably, this is not the only kind of family history we could write; but these standard computer print-out forms allow the historian tremendous flexibility and control.

SOURCES FOR THE NEAR FAMILY

There is a basic difference between the sources for the near family (one's immediate family, the family of one's personal experience and immediate memory) and sources for the far family (one's ancestral family, the one the writer never knew personally and which he accesses almost solely through historical documents). Obviously the shift in the kind of sources a writer will find available for the near family as opposed to the far family is gradual rather than distinct. The near family is the family of our personal and immediate memory, and it generates far more historical and primary-source documents and certainly far more personal artifacts than does the far family. It is often surprising how much material one accumulates and can use as the basis of a near-family history. As the researcher moves farther back into the past, though, he has fewer and fewer personal memories, artifacts, and photographs at his disposal and must rely more and more on historical documents alone. Eventually, the writer is left with little more than the name

Pedigree Overview. The pedigree overview is the most general or abstract chart. Its value lies in its capacity to display a simple and very general overview of the complete family line. The family historian can move quickly up and down and across various lines. Further, he can easily distinguish between geographic and cultural units as they relate to families, isolate familial subcultures, and contrast broad family value systems.

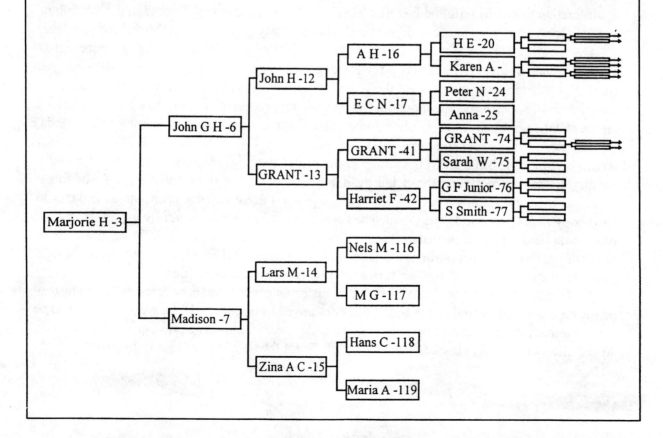

Family Group Sheet. This chart contains more detailed information and is less abstract than the pedigree overview, thus comprising a more specific level of information organization. While the writer cannot draw conclusions as abstract as he can with the pedigree overview, he can now isolate the details (notes for all members of any particular family are also available) that characterize one particular familial unit, linking and contrasting individual persons and family units.

Family Group Record—MRIN 30		
Wed., Jul 14, 1993		
Husband: Henry GOLDUP -57		
Born: ABT 1739	Place:	
Chr.:	Place:	
Marr.: ABT 1764	Place: Quebec	
Died: 1768	Place: Tryon River, Prince Edward I., Canada	
Bur.:	Place:	
Father:	Mother:	
Other Wives:		
Wife: Jane Mrs. -58		
Born: ABT 1743	Place:	
Chr.:	Place:	
Died: 1824	Place:	
Bur.:	Place:	
Father:	Mother:	
Other Husbands: William WARREN		
Sex Children	List each child (living or dead)	
M/F	in order of birth	
1. Name: John GOULDRUP -49	Spouse: Judith PARTRIDGE -50	
M Born: ABT 1765	Place: Quebec (?), Canada	
Chr.:	Place:	
Marr.: 8 MAY 1796	Place: Prince Edward I., Canada	
Died: 1843	Place: Tryon, Prince Edward I., Canada	
2. Name: Charlotte GOULDRUP -646	Spouse: John LORD -647	
F Born: 1768	Place: Prince Edward I., Canada	
Chr.:	Place:	
Marr.: 30 JUL 1787	Place: Tryon, Prince Edward I., Canada	
Died: 17 SEP 1842	Place: Tryon, Prince Edward I., Canada	
3. Name:	Spouse:	
Born:	Place:	
Chr.:	Place:	
Marr.:	Place:	
Died:	Place:	
4. Name:	Spouse:	
Born:	Place:	
Chr.:	Place:	
Marr.:	Place:	
Died:	Place:	

Name and address of submitter:
Dr. Lawrence P. Gouldrup
23812 Avenida Columbia
Mission Viejo, CA 92691
Phone: (714) 837-1316
Relationship of submitter to husband: _____ wife: _____

Individual Summary Chart. This chart is the least abstract and the most detailed of the three levels. Space does not allow me to include an example here; the notes alone run eight pages.

of an ancestor, a birth, marriage, or death date, and the place of the birth, marriage, or death; sometimes hardly that. These names, dates, and places then become the pedigree charts and family group sheets, which, in turn, become the only basis of far-family history.

Artifacts

One simple but effective technique of near-family prewriting is the artifactual approach. An artifact is technically a manufactured object such as a tool or an ornament, any natural object or substance that someone has altered or worked and left behind. Every family or local historian knows the value of artifacts in giving the story of the past a sense of authentic reality. The essence of the artifactual approach is to write with visual detail, with the eye fixed on the specific or particular: the ancient and silent building, the handwriting and spatial arrangement of the document, the comforts and mechanical features of the automobile, the color and surprises of the toy, the art and function of the curiously fashioned glass, and the fabric, color, construction, and style of antiquated clothing. Beatrix Potter—the creator of Peter Rabbit, Mr. Jeremy Fisher, and Mrs. Tiggy Winkle—perhaps because she was an artist first and a writer second, used the particular in her charming and universally popular stories. She would establish her pet animals— mice, rabbits, and hedgehogs—in and around her home, often keeping them in her own bedroom. There she would give them names, dress them, and place them in miniature doll-house settings. Watching their natural movements and noting their every detail and antic, she drew and made up stories which were absolutely true to the nature of the animal described.

> Many years later when commenting on one of Kenneth Grahame's books, Beatrix Potter wrote, "Yes—Kenneth Grahame ought to have been an artist—at least all writers for children ought to have a sufficient recognition of what things look like—did he not describe 'Toad' as combing his hair? A mistake to fly in the face of nature—A frog may wear galoshes; but I don't hold with toads having beards or wigs! So I prefer Badger." Therefore in all aspects of Mr. Jeremy Fisher's appearance and activities, he remains true to nature.
>
> — Leslie Linder, *A History of the Writings of Beatrix Potter Including Unpublished Work*

There is something remarkably true to nature about a frog or toad wearing galoshes and not having hair. Yet this obvious extension of the amphibian's natural physical characteristics would occur only to someone who had taken the time to observe the frog carefully. It is also remarkable how readers such as children, completely unsophisticated as to man's complex world, immediately know the difference between a frog which wears galoshes and one which combs his hair. Her technique was so simple it was flawless.

The artifactual approach to writing can be effective in producing family history that will have the ring of truth, that the reader will find as authentic. In chapter 3 of *WFN*, I begin with characterization because many find it easier to conceptualize a personality first and to see that character in action and time, second. (See *WFN* 61–64.) One of the easiest ways to visualize a character—contemporary or historical—is to gather pictures and artifacts that relate to that ancestor or relative; then arrange, interpret, and write about the pictures, landscape, buildings, and artifacts with which those near relatives were involved. For example, if you write your autobiography or the biography of a relative near in time, you can expect to have numerous pictures and artifacts. Gather them together and arrange the items chronologically beginning with the very earliest such as baby shoes or baby books. Then you might turn to early report cards, boy scout badges, and pictures. And on to adulthood. Or arrange items according to a category or type such as rocks, shells, bottle caps, or flowers you collected while on a family vacation one summer. The point is to see, handle, and feel the historical items that make up the history you are writing, much as Beatrix Potter watched a frog long enough to know that it could have galoshes and not hair. If you remain true to what you see, you will never be in danger of writing a history that is forced and faked.

Exercise 2-1

Take either a family group sheet or an individual summary complete with notes and make a list of the artifacts in your possession that relate directly or indirectly to that family or individual. Name the family or individual and list the artifacts:

NAME OF FAMILY OR INDIVIDUAL:

ARTIFACTS IN YOUR POSSESSION

1. _____

2. _____

3. _____

4. _____

5. _____

6. _____

7. _____

8. _____

9. _____

10. _____

Now group the various artifacts into types or categories such as an event (graduation, marriage, birth of a child), person (parent, sibling, aunt), place (a specific house or building, work, play area), or time (childhood, youth, military service, employment). For example, you may group into one category several artifacts that relate to your mother: her glasses, some scribbled notes that she left as she lay dying, a watch that you gave her, her gilded baby shoes. When you've grouped all the artifacts, go back and describe how each item differs from other members of the same category. Be specific as to construction, purpose, color, age, texture, size, cost.

CATEGORY 1:

a. _____

Distinguishing characteristics: _____

_____

b. _____

Distinguishing characteristics: _____

_____

c. _____

Distinguishing characteristics: _____

_____

CATEGORY 2:

a. _____

Distinguishing characteristics: _____

_____

b. _____

Distinguishing characteristics: _____

_____

c. _____

Distinguishing characteristics: _____

_____

CATEGORY 3:

a. _____

Distinguishing characteristics: _____

_____

b. _____

Distinguishing characteristics: _____

_____

c. _____

Distinguishing characteristics: _____

_____

CATEGORY 4: _____

a. _____

Distinguishing characteristics: _____

_____

b. _____

Distinguishing characteristics: _____

_____

c. _____

Distinguishing characteristics: _____

_____

Lists of Documents

When I began preparing my own near-family history, I easily came up with the following list of family documents:

1. Tape recordings of family activities
   a. Reel-to-reel tapes of family discussions
   b. Mini- and regular cassettes of various trips: Israel and Great Britain
   c. Videos of family activities:
      (1) Trip to San Francisco
      (2) Holidays such as Thanksgiving and Christmas
      (3) Family reunions

2. Journals and diaries

    a. My journals

        (1) Journal of my freshman and sophomore years at college, 1954–56

        (2) My LDS mission to Germany, 1956–59

        (3) My junior year in college, marriage and first year of married life, 1959–1962

        (4) Brief entries, 1980–81

    b. My daughter Lindsay's journals

    c. My wife Sandy's journals

    d. My son Mark's journals

    e. My son Stephen's journals

3. Letters

    a. Letters my wife wrote to her family while we lived in Saudi Arabia

    b. Letters which various relatives wrote us

4. Film

    a. Family photographs

    b. Slides from my LDS mission

    c. Family slides

        (1) Saudi Arabia

        (2) Britain

5. Personal files on each family member

    a. School records

    b. Vital records

    c. Honors

    d. Academic activities

6. Business files

    a. Travel records

        (1) Ashland, Oregon, Shakespeare Festival

        (2) Great Britain

        (3) Balkans

        (4) Salt Lake City genealogy trips

        (5) Soviet Union

    b. IRS records

7. Miscellaneous family files

    a. Publications

    b. Insurance: health, dental, automobile, house

    c. Medical and dental histories

d. Various church activities

e. Papers I wrote in school

f. Property records

g. Purchases: furnace, automobiles, electronic equipment, solar device, swimming pool

Exercise 2-2

Make your own list of sources that you might use in writing your personal near-family history.

_____

_____

_____

_____

_____

_____

_____

_____

_____

_____

_____

_____

_____

_____

_____

_____

_____

_____

_____

_____

SOURCES FOR THE FAR FAMILY

Letters, Journals, and Diaries

Many family historians begin with a journal or a diary which is, as the word suggests, the record of an individual periodically or by date of activity. The only ordering strategy is chronology; as it happened, someone recorded it. As you read a journal, make observations and synthesize the various journal notations or primary source documents in a notebook.

Letters, journals, and diaries reveal the true character of both the near and far family. A good example is a letter my wife wrote years ago. Not long ago I came across this letter , one she had written to me a few weeks before we married. There was a certain innocence about the letter, an enthusiasm which I felt had disappeared from her personality over the years. I was troubled with my observation and discussed it with her it at length. We concluded that she had grown increasingly protective of her girl-like enthusiasm and less willing to express it as I had vacillated over our years of marriage between high points of tender passion and low points of pouting silence. While our relationship had grown and we had become better adjusted, she had learned to deal with my mood of silence by keeping her feelings to herself. Her personality, which was far more even than mine, could only thrive in a very even emotional environment, not in an environment characterized by swings from excitement to depression. My broad personal enthusiasm had intrigued and attracted her as we dated, but she had found my emotional swings difficult to live with. Her evenness and emotional stability had attracted me as a tempering and reassuring anchor, but I too had had difficulty with what I interpreted as a lack of enthusiasm and genuine love. I noted these observations, then, in my notebook with certain quotes from the actual letters and journals which we had both kept.

As you read, there are several things you can do to make what you read more valuable to your writing.

COLLECT QUOTES

First, record quotes from the books and journals that have interested and impressed you. Consider the bibliographies in *WFN* chapter 2, and when you come across something that you find relevant or interesting, write it down or note it in your computer record. Underline key words and phrases.

One of my distant family members, John Grant, worked as a locksmith in Willenhall, England, during the mid-1800s. While I had read his descriptions of his craft, I could never form much of a mental picture of what it meant to be a locksmith until I came across a description complete with pictures of the Locksmith Working Museum in *In Britain*:

John Hodson and his son used to busy themselves in the workshop with his wife and daughters helping them out as well as running a draper's shop in the front-room of their home in Willenhall. Now this cozy arrangement of two thriving businesses is permanently on show as The Lock Museum. Recently opened after two years' work on the Victorian house and backyard workshop, 54 New Road typifies all that is best in a local museum, paying tribute to a long-established town industry and supported by enthusiastic volunteers, ready to don costumes and work as demonstrators in the workshop, which produces bar-padlocks just as Mr. Hodson did at the turn of the century, and which the museum shop now sells as souvenirs. The Hodson family had been making locks in the town since 1792, moving to New Road in 1904, and <u>Willenhall has been the centre of Britain's lockmaking industry since the Industrial Revolution. By 1850 there were as many as 300 lock workshops</u> —today only about eighty remain.

— In Britain

I made a copy of the article which I filed under John Grant; but more importantly, I quoted the above passage in a notebook which I am keeping on John Grant, underlining the portions indicated above. It is important that you as a writer do more than simply file a quote. What is filed is soon forgotten, but underlining a quote makes it a working part of your notebook. Remember, we are learning how to write, not how to file.

READ AND RESPOND

Second, read and respond. As you read provocative or interesting statements, quote the statement and add your reflections. Argue with and suggest alternatives.

DEVELOP BACKGROUND LISTS

Third, develop background lists as you read. Establish the general historical trends, geographic features, linguistic patterns, economic trends, and political changes of the area from which your family comes. Consult an encyclopedia article on the background of the area and compile an initial bibliography. You will probably have to consult several articles in the encyclopedia, but if you take a few hours before diving into the complexities of a good academic library, you will have a feel for the directions in which you want to conduct research.

Local Libraries

Many libraries now have on-line catalog systems, some limited to the specific library and some accessing vast databases that take into account all the libraries in a certain state or region. The LDS Family History Library's catalog is available in local LDS family history centers throughout the United States. In Utah, the UNIS system is limited to the holdings at the University of Utah. In California, the Melvyl on-line catalog currently lists approximately six million books at libraries on all University of California campuses and over 600,000 periodical titles owned by the libraries of all University of California and California State University campuses, Cal Tech, Stanford, USC, The Getty Center for the History of Art and the Humanities, and the Center for Research Libraries. Other databases such as the OCLC (Online Computer Library Center) access library collections by region specifically for the purpose of interlibrary loan and are not available to patrons; contact a reference librarian for help.

Local History Societies

One of the most important steps that the family historian can take is to join a local historical society. Eakle and Cerny's *The Source* has a list which provides a starting point: "Appendix C: Historical Societies and Agencies in the United States." Angus Baxter in his *In Search of Your British and Irish Roots* provides similar lists for all the shires. Many of these societies publish journals which contain articles of local interest, articles which we would find in no major library.

Area-Specific Libraries

Ultimately, you will have to consult libraries located in the geographic region about which you are writing. While Melvyl lists approximately two hundred titles on Bas-Rhin (Alsace), few of the books are helpful, and in conducting my personal historical research, I determined that there was no source in the United States for the name of an historical society in the northern section of Bas-Rhin. The result was a trip to France, where I spoke to as many local genealogists and family historians as I could find and where I bought current publications on Bas-Rhin; after consulting the bibliographies in these books and visiting local genealogical and academic libraries, I found hundreds of titles that are not available in the United States. I also located an historical society which publishes a journal, *L'Outre-Foret*; I promptly subscribed. This journal concerns itself with the northern section of Bas-Rhin (Alsace), the area from which the main part of my family came. In the process, I was able to make the acquaintance of several Alsatian historians who were extremely warm and enthusiastic about my project.

As I read, I isolated numerous general facts which began to give historical meaning to the facts of my pedigree charts and family group sheets:

1. The terrible destructions of the 1600s in Alsace
   a. The Thirty Years War
   b. The pacification of Alsace by Louis XIV
   c. The War of Spanish Succession
2. The repopulation policies of Louis XIV with the greatest influx of foreign persons after the end of the War of Spanish Succession in 1714
3. The agricultural revolution of the 1700s
   a. Change from a subsistence to a commercial agriculture
   b. The development of population pressures
   c. Inflation and financial pressures
4. The growth of political instability leading up to the French Revolution
   a. Individual versus communal property rights
   b. The deterioration of the peasants' situation
   c. The hunger for land
   d. Economic crash of 1788–1789
   e. The French Revolution and Napoleon

5. The period of abandonment: the first half of the nineteenth century

    a. Population pressures

    b. Natural disasters

    c. Emotional crises

These facts fit well with what I knew about my family: first, that formal records concerning my family began toward the end of the 1600s, actually between 1650 and 1700; and second, that three specific branches of the family (one Bavarian, one Swiss, and one probably Italian) had arrived in Alsace shortly after 1700. Then during the ensuing century, the Dauer family achieved relative economic prosperity with numerous members of the family participating as artisans in the economic recovery. The family multiplied and grew faster than the negative pressures of infant mortality and natural death patterns, and this increase in population contributed to the growing demand for more land. Then, the political and economic chaos that preceded and accompanied the French Revolution and the Napoleonic era and the natural disasters which taxed the human spirit were directly responsible for my ancestors' leaving Alsace in the 1830s for New York. Finally, what was fascinating and surfaced clearly when I merged the genealogical record with what I know about general Alsatian circumstances was that attitudes and patterns which my ancestors exhibited in America were simply a transference of needs and emotions developed in the Old World: their hunger for land, their rising level of economic expectation, and their drive for personal and emotional fulfillment. My Alsatian history begins with the need for land setting my ancestors in movement and ends with that same need transferring my ancestors to America.

PREWRITING EXERCISES

WRITING ABOUT ARTIFACTS

An artifact can be a window into a person's past. As we all do, one writer who grew up in California had gathered objects from events, people, and places that had meant a great deal to her, and one item that was particularly valuable was a gold-leaf wedding tea set. Each summer when she visited her grandparents in Idaho Falls, her childless aunt would invite her to a special tea party. Her parents as well as her grandparents never allowed her to drink real tea, but this aunt would not only provide exotic sandwiches, cookies, and chocolates, but real tea at these "scandalous" tea parties; and after each tea party, her aunt would take her down to the railroad tracks where together they would place pennies on the rails, wait like bandits in the bushes, and watch the wonderful effects of a several-ton train on a Lincoln penny. One day not long before it was evident that this writer was growing a bit old for tea parties and when it was looking as if boys back in California would be more important in summer than grandparents and aunts in Idaho, this aunt asked the writer to put her name on the one object in her whole house that she would like to have when the aunt died. The young girl, of course, picked the wedding tea set. Years later when the aunt died, someone going through her belongings found a note on the tea set, and contacted the writer. One day in a writing class, I asked the students each to bring an artifact to class, and of course, this writer brought the tea set, laden with memories. The story she told and later wrote to fulfill the assignment was so laden with emotion that there was hardly a tearless eye in the class. One way to write a story is to use an artifact as the mechanism for moving back into the past.

Exercise 2-3

Consider how an artifact might be the basis of a good story by analyzing the artifact in terms of meaning in your life or the lives of your ancestors.

THE ARTIFACT:

MEMORIES ASSOCIATED WITH THE ARTIFACT

1. _____

2. _____

3. _____

4. _____

5. _____

6. _____

7. _____

Another exercise that I have found to be very useful for beginning writers is the draw-a-picture approach. In fact, Dan Wakefield has published in his book *The Story of Your Life: Writing a Spiritual Autobiography* a series of exercises that literally walk a writer from his childhood, through his adolescence, past important guides and friends, to an analysis of one's entire life journey. One does not have to be a competent artist to make this method work. One student I had drew a picture of the home of his earliest memory: his bed and bedroom, the kitchen, the backyard, the living room. Then he walked himself through each of these rooms, jotted down memories and events, and eventually fashioned those memories into a story about his early childhood. He could not have prevented the memories from flowing onto paper if he had wanted to. People and events long forgotten suddenly came alive out of a simple, crude sketch of his childhood home. The technique is really very simple: sketch a home, a friend, yourself, a parent. Then jot down the memories.

The following is a student's story about a chair:

A Chair Called Horace

First-time visitors to the Harold Little home sometimes comment about the unusual chair in a corner of the living room, whereupon they are introduced to "Horace." Horace is a family heirloom, a platform rocker, that is always handed down to the oldest son in the family. This is a "tradition" that began when John received the chair at the death of his father, George, in 1933. The tradition is rather puzzling because John was the third oldest son in his father's family. The story goes that George had five sons and three daughters. When George died, there were five items of value to be given to the sons. Each son chose the item he wanted. John, with his wife's coaching, decided on the chair because it once belonged to an ancestor who ran for president in 1872—Horace Greeley. The chair is certainly worthy of note. The seat is low to the floor and covered with a piece of tooled leather that was applied about 1970. The elongated back with its eleven slender, bowed spindles is framed by 38-inch side-posts firmly fastened into the base and extending seven inches above the head-piece. It is armless. The intricacies of the motion-enabling mechanism are partly hidden behind a framework spaced with short, turned posts, five on each side. Further investigation reveals a suspension system made of iron, which produces not a rocking motion but a gliding one. Its varnished surface gleams.

Now an example written about a pair of glasses:

When my mother died, my Aunt Lee somehow remembered to save my mother's glasses from certain loss and later presented them to me in a small box. It was an act of kindness that only she could have understood. I was not present at the time of my mother's death, and my sister, in a pattern that she had followed for years, had managed to confiscate all articles of value. My aunt had alone taken the time to save a pair of glasses that I am certain my mother would never have wanted to take with her to the grave. My mother was very near-sighted, and she shared in that feeling common to her time that glasses were somehow a mark of physical inferiority. The reason I was so aware of my mother's glasses was because I had inherited her myopia. My father never wore glasses. In fact, glasses seemed to link me to my mother in a way that I was both proud and terribly ashamed of. I was a bookish lad; the glasses insured that. I was always four-eyes and seemed to feel more comfortable playing off by myself than engaging in rough boyhood games which posed a constant threat to my glasses. And my mother was always worrying herself about my breaking my glasses. I can remember as a young boy noticing the style of glasses that my mother wore. Earlier in her life, she had worn small glasses with small, dark rims completely around the glasses, but later in life she took to wearing glasses that had only a rim across the top with the lower edges of the eyeglass exposed. There was a time when I wanted to have glasses just like hers, a fact that still troubles me as I was keenly aware that I related much more to my mother than to my father. Later on when contacts became possible, it was my Aunt Lee who helped me buy my first pair of contacts, a grueling experience. My eyes would water and be constantly red, but with a determination born of years of emotional trauma I persisted. When I married, I quickly gave up the contacts; and when soft contacts became available a few years later, I bought myself a pair. However I was careless in cleaning the soft lenses and eventually acquired a disease in the right eye that to this day threatens my vision.

The purpose of these artifactual exercises is to allow a physical object to stimulate your memory so that you can recall as many details from your past as possible. The theory is that if you worry about punctuation, grammar, and style, your brain becomes clogged and dysfunctional—writer's block. Start with the physical object, the artifact from the past: the picture, the baby shoe, the graduation certificate, the boy scout badge—and jot down associated memories. Be indiscriminate! Make no attempt to edit or correct ideas and images as they come. Write as much as you wish and as often as you wish. Stop when you are tired, and then resume your writing when something interesting comes to your mind.

Exercise 2-4

Pick an artifact from your past and write about it, without editing, in a brief paragraph.

_____

_____

_____

_____

_____

_____

_____

_____

_____

_____

_____

WRITING FROM LISTS

Explore Your Memory to Develop Lists

In recent years, several writers have produced books which are really lists of potential writing topics. Two are Patricia Ann Case's *How to Write Your Autobiography* and Jeanne Pittman's

My Personal History Workbook. Even though these kinds of workbooks do not use the artifactual approach, they are very helpful, particularly to beginning writers. Pittman's book presents a series of questions with blanks which the writer fills in; these questions are often very specific, but almost all of them could easily evoke a series of associated memories.

SCHOOL DAYS

I started school at _____ School, in _____ (city) at age _____.

Other elementary schools I attended were _____ School, from _____

to _____, and _____ School, from _____ to _____.

My first feelings about starting school were _____.

Later my feelings were _____.

Case's book is similar.

TEEN YEARS

1. Did your family celebrate birthdays?

2. How did they celebrate birthdays?

3. Was there any special celebration for any of your teenage birthdays?

4. How did you feel about becoming a teenager?

5. What was expected of you as a teenager?

6. Did you attend high school?

7. If so, what high school did you attend?

8. Describe how that high school appeared to you.

9. Where was your high school?

And so on. Each of these questions or statements with fill-in blanks is clearly a prod to writing. As such, they are what most writing books call *topic lists*. They provide subjects and areas in which the writer can explore his memory. It is just as easy for you to make your own topic lists, however. Pittman and Case's workbooks provide good starting points, but obviously as you make these lists, particularly when working from an artifact or photograph, you will discover in your own past scores of topics that will provide excellent starting points for further writing.

Exercise 2-5

Now develop your own lists. State a topic, a phase in your life, an age, a challenge, or a name, and then list the items that come to mind.

TOPIC, PHASE IN YOUR LIFE, AGE, OBJECT, ETC.:

ITEMS THAT COME TO MIND:

1. _____

2. _____

3. _____

4. _____

5. _____

6. _____

7. _____

8. _____

9. _____

10. _____

Artifactual Topic Lists

Make a list of all the artifacts or topics associated with those artifacts that you might like to explore. Reread your list to inspire new ideas or topics. Jot them down. Leave the list for a period of time, and when you return, refresh your memory as to what you have written. Or ignore what you have written and, considering the artifacts or pictures, let new topics come to mind. The purpose of an artifactual topic list is to provide you with topics or subjects which you might want to consider later or make entries about in your notebook.

Exercise 2-6

List artifacts associated with your far-family below, and then list any new topic ideas that the artifact list might inspire.

ARTIFACT:

TOPICS:

1. _____

2. _____

3. _____

ARTIFACT:

TOPICS:

1. _____

2. _____

3. _____

ARTIFACT:

TOPICS:

1. _____

2. _____

3. _____

ARTIFACT:

TOPICS:

1. _____

2. _____

3. _____

Brainstorming

Brainstorming is another way of working from a topics list. After you have selected a topic from the topic list, list everything that comes to mind as you think about the topic. Make no attempt to edit or control what you are writing on the paper; that will come later. Should you find it difficult to think of something, use a series of exploration questions such as who, what, when, where, why, and how. It even works to brainstorm in groups, for example with a relative who has experienced the same memories with you.

The following are examples from students. Notice the natural progression and association of ideas with ideas, particularly in the second example :

CAR-HOP JOB

cold	tricky trays
$12.50 a week	juke box
uniform	feet
some sights in some cars	boss' accusation
only 18 and should have been 21	

U.S. ARMY

West Germany	Alabama	Texas	North Carolina	South Carolina
guard duty	1st armor	C.I.D.s	hospital	military police
top secret	officer	dream	psychologist	train
pubs	exam	civilian	sergeant	assault
investigations	poetry/book	roommate	witness	

Now let's look at some exploration questions. A student submitted the following after coming across a picture of her grandfather's mobile home, or "housecar" as she calls it.

GRANDPA'S HOUSECAR

Who:

Grandpa was a tall man — 6'1"

white curly hair when I knew him

wore a mustache, like Mark Twain's mustache

was a hunter, fisherman, blacksmith, rancher

worked with the Indians (knew Chief Joseph)

helped Dr. Wheeler on the Fort Hall, Idaho, Indian reservation with the Indians (1909-1915)

loved to read Mark Twain

What:

>car was a curiosity
>
>new, strange to many people
>
>car was a Ford with a special body
>
>Grandpa could not stand up in the housecar
>
>side of car could be pushed out

Where:

>he parked the car in our backyard quite often
>
>Long Beach earthquake in March, 1933; buildings destroyed all around us; we stayed in tents and in the housecar until aftershocks were over and utilities were restored

When:

>I found 1928 registration paper for Grandpa's, pink slip
>
>found his 1942 driver's license, yellow paper

How:

>took his beloved fox terrier with him on trips
>
>brought home gold nuggets and rattlers from rattlesnakes he had killed
>
>Grandpa cooked on his stove in the housecar for us; creamed onions were his specialty

Why:

>Grandpa traveled all over California and much of Mexico in the housecar

Clustering

Clustering is like brainstorming; only with clustering you show the relationship between ideas. Let us suppose that you are considering a family home. The procedure is shown in figure 2-4. Drawing first a small balloon or circle in the center of a blank sheet of paper, write the expression "family home" inside the circle. Related to the "family home" is the idea of "chores," which you write inside another balloon or circle above or below the circled "family home" on the same piece of paper. You connect these balloons or circles with a line. You then connect the balloon "chores" with a series of ballooned or circled ideas such as "drinking lemonade in summer," "watching out for rattlesnakes," "wanting to escape to the river." Returning now to the original balloon, "family home," you draw another line off another direction to a new balloon or circle with "school" inside the circle, continuing on to connect ballooned or circled ideas such as "walking through the pasture," "one-room schoolhouse," and "drawing drinking water from a well" to the circled "school." The purpose is both to generate ideas easily as well as to show the relationships between one major idea such as "family home," secondary ideas such as "chores" and "school," and related subideas.

Example of the clustering method.

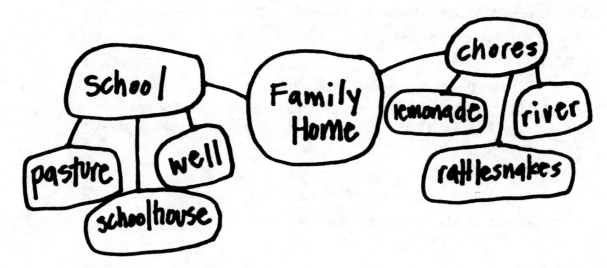

Exercise 2-7

Now try representing some of your memories with the clustering method:

Freewriting

Freewriting, perhaps the easiest way of working from an artifactual topics list, is the beginning stage of what is called the personal essay. What starts out as spontaneous freewriting will, with editing and revisions, end up being the personal essay. Pick a topic from your topic list or even an artifact or picture of some person or object out of your past and write down, without stopping, whatever comes to your mind about the person or item. Make no attempt to edit or change anything that you write. Above all, do not correct your grammar or worry about your spelling. The only control is that you write down anything and everything that comes to mind about one topic or artifact. Do not stray from the announced topic or artifact.

Most family historians are familiar with the Scandinavian farm histories. Agnes Rothery, who wrote several years ago, used a technique similar to freewriting/personal essay in her book *A Fitting Habitation* where she recorded her family history as it grew out of and was associated with the houses she and her husband had occupied.

The following personal essay, now polished and edited, began as a piece of freewriting. The author wrote down every memory associated with the family car. Later, when she polished the freewriting, she eliminated some memories and arranged all items chronologically. For some, these personal essays are the final product. But for the serious family writer, these personal essays are sources for an expanded exposition, or scenes or episodes in a more ambitious narrative.

Buick

Buick was grey . . . a plain, utilitarian grey . . . not a convertible . . . no leather top . . . no jaunty spare tire on the back . . . not even a thin strip of color anywhere. Just grey. It cost $1000.

Franklin Johnson was a field inspector and had just returned from a year on the New York docks, sent by Sunkist to learn the shipping end of the citrus industry. He purchased Buick on the way home. It conformed to Sunkist's rule in every way. His assets were many. While most of them were physical . . . handsome . . . a good disposition . . . a background of stability . . . and he liked me, others were tangible . . . a permanent position with Sunkist Growers, which necessitated a move every four months (and I liked that), a modest bank account, and Buick, entirely paid for.

During our courtship he was working in Ventura and when he came south on weekends, we had a lovely shaded hill somewhere in Riverside where we would always drive to watch the city lights and talk and talk . . . alone. One night we heard a slight rustle and look up to a very sullen and frightening-looking man. He stood on Franklin's side and suddenly another equally disgusting-looking person was on my side. They just stood there and Franklin asked what they wanted . . . they didn't answer . . . then I noticed a swift movement of Franklin's arm, the starter ground into life and Buick leapt forward, scattering the men and shot down the hill and back into civilization. You can guess we never returned, but we discussed many times the horrifying list of "what if's."

September 9, 1939 Buick was washed and carefully polished and loaded with brand new luggage. It transported us to All Saints Episcopal Church where we were married at high noon. After the ceremony at the altar we walked outside and talked with our friends and Reverend Henry Smith for a few moments and then drove off in Buick. About three blocks from the church Franklin remembered he had failed to give the rector the small white envelope tucked into the breast pocket of his jacket. We turned back and as we came to the church we found everyone was still standing there visiting. With a red face he got out of Buick and gave Reverend Smith the envelope and once more we started off.

Two years after our marriage, Franklin left Sunkist to take over the citrus groves at Glen Ivy for his mother. We moved to the ranch at Glen Ivy, which was ten miles from everywhere. Buick soon learned the way to Corona through repetition.

In 1941 . . . June . . . Buick took us to the Riverside Community Hospital on a fast and anxious trip where our daughter, Kristin, was born. In those days new mothers could stay in the hospital two weeks, and then could stay with the grandmothers for two more weeks. Buick made the trip daily. We paid our pediatrician monthly to watch over this precious little girl and whenever I felt I needed a wiser head to explain each new development associated with her well-being Buick took us to his office. In 1943, another anxious trip to Riverside Community Hospital and this time it was a boy, Ray. However, this time we didn't have to make so many trips to the pediatrician since I was getting the hang of being a mother.

World War II was now threatening our freedom, our young men, and the casual use of commodities . . . food, fuel, and man-power. Inasmuch as Franklin was now classified as a farmer, Buick became accustomed to travelling on tractor gasoline . . . which was abundant when our ration stamps were gone.

Buick was a girl scout and went to all the meetings and to summer camp at Arrowhead. Buick was also a cub scout and went to all the meetings and to summer camp somewhere in the mountains.

When the boys were of junior high age, they started school at Army and Navy Academy in Carlsbad. Buick learned the way there, too. It patiently waited beside the parade ground during dress parades and soccer games, and it transported homesick cadets to nearby restaurants when they couldn't handle the Academy food a second longer. In the spring of Ray's junior year at the Academy we had a telephone call from a hospital in Oceanside, and we were told Ray had been admitted the night before . . . they had run some test and could we come down. He had been home for Easter the week before and seemed to be well . . . so you can imagine how anxious we were.

After a brief, but devastating consultation with the doctor, we learned that the diagnosis was cancer. Have you ever felt as if some enormous vise was literally squeezing your heart our of your body?

The next day we three drove in Buick to Los Angeles to see Dr. Mahlon, the cancer specialist. Innumerable tests and consultations confirmed the original diagnosis, and the x-ray treatments were started, and the waiting . . . and hoping . . . and praying, in spite of the fact that we were told it was unlikely that Ray had more than four months to live.

Buick transported us every single day for those four months over the busy freeways between Corona and Los Angeles . . . then on a hot and muggy day in August it was over. Buick was parked near the entrance to St. John's Episcopal Church where our family and friends and the entire corps of cadets from the academy helped us, as best they could, commit Ray's soul to the ultimate glory.

This venerable old car bore the dust and scratches and dings with dignity and it never suffered the indignities of being scraped or repainted. Perhaps one of the last tasks was carrying load after load of clothing and small household necessities from the ranch to our large home on Grand Boulevard in Corona. Finally, it suffered total separation on a used car lot in Elsinore. It had been replaced by yet another Buick, but our involvement with any car has never again been so personal and for seventeen years.

— Dorothy Johnson

THE NONFICTIONAL EXPOSITION

STEP ONE: LIMIT THE TOPIC OR SUBJECT

Every piece of expository writing must have some kind of purpose or reason for being. All too often, beginning family history writers write without any focus or direction. Literally they meander from subject to subject. This kind of meandering interests only the writer and confuses the reader; to communicate effectively, it is imperative that the writer limit his subject and make some kind of a point.

Chapter 2 of *WFN* deals with patterns or limited subjects that emerge naturally from historical documents: where the family came from and where and why it settled where it did; how the family earned its money and how it spent that money; what the family considered important or valuable; and what kind of social standing and personality patterns the family exhibited. Many more patterns or subjects will suggest themselves as you work through the genealogical data, but unless you as a writer limit yourself to a particular subject, you will wander from idea to idea. There are two steps in limiting your topic or subject.

First, determine general historical topics. Initially, it is best to see the section of the pedigree chart that you plan to write about as the history of a dominant family. The time period under consideration, available historical records, migrational patterns, and the length of residence in a certain locality will determine which family on the pedigree chart you will choose. In the case of my Alsatian ancestors, there were several families that intermarried and bound their lives together, yet it was the Dauer family that seemed to weave through and form the basis of all these familial changes. Individuals migrated from Germany, Switzerland, and possibly even Italy to settle in the area of Lauterbourg, Alsace, France, and it was into the large and stable Lauterbourg Dauer family that they married.

Second, if there are particular topics or incidents that emerge about a certain individual, individuals, or families, establish patterns that themselves can become the focal points or limited subjects of expositions. As you consider any pedigree chart, stories leap out of the barren records. It is fascinating to leaf through the records considering how often women gave birth: the normal rate seems to be a child every two years. There is the cold statistic of the death of the mother two short weeks after the birth of the child, probably from infection associated with childbirth. And suddenly there is a subject or topic: women who two and one-half centuries ago gave life and struggled for life in a world where medicine belonged far more to superstition than to science.

Exercise 2-8

The first step in writing an exposition is to limit oneself to topics about which there is sufficient information for the writer to develop a detailed exposition. Now consider a person or a family that you are writing about; jot down several topics about which you might be able to gather enough information to write short expositions:

FAMILY OR INDIVIDUAL:

Topic 1:_____

_____

_____

Topic 2: _____

_____

_____

Topic 3: _____

_____

_____

Topic 4: _____

_____

_____

STEP TWO: ORGANIZE YOUR IDEAS

The next step involves planning the organization of your ideas. The method of organization is normally termed a *rhetorical device* or *strategy*. I have selected each of the historical situations below from my own family history. The topic is how I narrowed the historical situation, and the strategy describes how I might organize my exposition.

ITEM 1

    Situation: Henry Goldrup enlisted in the 2nd Battalion of the Royal American Regiment in 1757, was transported from Philadelphia in April 1758, to Halifax, Nova Scotia, fought in the Battle of Louisburg in the summer of 1758 and the Battle for Quebec in 1959, and was mustered out of the service in 1762.

    Topic: Life as a British soldier in the 2nd Battalion of the Royal American Regiment during the French and Indian War.

    Strategy: Describe the daily conditions of a British soldier.

ITEM 2

    Situation: In the late nineteenth century, William Grant spent twenty months in prison for polygamy. He suffered greatly from the difficult conditions, aggravated health problems, and separation from his family.

    Topic: William Grant's prison sentence.

    Strategy: Give examples of William Grant's difficult prison term.

ITEM 3

    Situation: Joseph Antoine Waller in the 1850s found opportunity and wealth in his new land holdings in Wisconsin, while his sisters and their husbands suffered from the natural disasters plaguing Alsace, France.

    Topic: Life in Wisconsin in the 1850s and in Alsace, France.

    Strategy: Compare or contrast life in Wisconsin and Alsace, France in the 1850s.

ITEM 4

    Situation: William Grant's life was characterized by various problems. He suffered personal health problems, business difficulties with creditors and clients, feelings of rejection from his church and neighbors, legal trials, and intense personal tragedies.

    Topic: William Grant's problems.

    Strategy: Classify William Grant's problems.

ITEM 5

Situation: William Grant gradually slipped from a fairly healthy psychological state to a condition of deep depression. The decline was brought on by many factors not the least of which was the thwarting of Grant's obsessive need for success and glory.

Topic: William Grant's depression.

Strategy: Delineate the causes of William Grant's depression.

Exercise 2-9

Take the same topics that you recorded in exercise 2-8 and devise a strategy or method of organization for each.

Strategy for Topic 1: _____

_____

_____

_____

_____

Strategy for Topic 2: _____

_____

_____

_____

_____

Strategy For Topic 3: _____

_____

_____

_____

_____

Strategy for Topic 4: _____

_____

_____

_____

_____

STEP THREE: DEVELOP A MAIN POINT—CONSTRUCT A THESIS

Now we must construct the topic as a *thesis*, a statement which states what you plan to establish or prove about the subject. The strategy that you have chosen will have a direct bearing on the thesis sentence. Let us begin with the easiest method of organization, the example exposition.

A thesis always has an argumentative edge. Many teachers of basic composition courses ask their students to frame a thesis by completing the sentence "The purpose of this paper is to prove (to convince, show, or establish for the reader) that . . . ." The process consists of two steps:

> a. Complete the sentence, "The purpose of this paper is to prove to the reader that William Grant's prison term was difficult."

> b. Now drop the first part of the sentence: William Grant's prison term was difficult.

It is best to think of a thesis as a complete sentence composed of two parts: the subject—"William Grant's prison term"—and the controlling idea or predicate—"was difficult." The predicate functions as the controlling idea. Thus when we actually write the paper, we are going to include only those events, qualities, and persons that will establish one and only one idea: the difficulty of William Grant's prison term. We are not interested in whether or not Grant provided well for his family, was a dedicated member of his church, or sent his two wives roses on each of their birthdays. It is important to remember this one simple fact since it is normally on this and this point alone that most writers of exposition go astray. They assume that they can include anything about William Grant in the exposition, and as a result, the paper wanders and lacks basic unity. By the rules which the writer of the thesis has imposed on herself, she is allowed only to discuss the difficult prison term.

Exercise 2-10

Try your hand at writing theses by completing these sentences for each topic you established in exercise 2-8.

TOPIC 1:

The purpose of this paper is to . . .

convince the reader that: _____

_____

_____

persuade the reader that: _____

_____

_____

establish for the reader that: _____

_____

_____

TOPIC 2:

The purpose of this paper is to . . .

convince the reader that: _____

_____

_____

persuade the reader that: _____

_____

_____

establish for the reader that: _____

_____

_____

TOPIC 3:

The purpose of this paper is to . . .

    convince the reader that: _____

_____

_____

    persuade the reader that: _____

_____

_____

    establish for the reader that: _____

_____

_____

TOPIC 4:

The purpose of this paper is to . . .

    convince the reader that: _____

_____

_____

    persuade the reader that: _____

_____

_____

    establish for the reader that: _____

_____

_____

While many writers organize their expositions around a thesis, normally an example thesis, often they may not explicitly state that thesis.

Wallace Stegner's "Letter—Much Too Late" in Carolyn Anthony's *Family Portraits* is an example of this. Stegner does not state the thesis explicitly although he implies it: "My mother cheerfully made the best of a dismal, cheerless life." He supports this thesis with several subideas: she saw the best in her son Wallace, she survived a youth of social deprivation and backbreaking labor, and she endured a humiliating marriage. In his conclusion, he comes back to his thesis:

> "All you can do is try," you used to tell me when I was scared of undertaking something. You got me to undertake many things I would not have dared undertake without your encouragement. You also taught me how to take defeat when it came, and it was bound to now and then. You taught me that if it hadn't killed me it was probably good for me.

> — Wallace Stegner, "Letter—Much Too Late"

Other writers explicitly state the thesis. Consider Mary Higgins Clark's "The 'F' Is For Fascinating," also in Carolyn Anthony's *Family Portraits* : Clark's thesis is clearly that her husband was fascinating. She supports this thesis with subideas: "He led his class in every subject every year." "A war hero, he came home covered in glory." "The Donald Trump of his day, his rise in the business world was meteoric. Well, as a matter of fact, it wasn't." "He was a husband and father beyond comparison." "His wife had a dream and he encouraged that dream." "He was an inspiration to all who knew him." "He is always with us." "We shall meet him in the hereafter." And she develops each of these subideas in paragraphs with details from his life. Everything in the exposition, the paragraphs filled with details, support the subideas, which in turn support and establish the thesis.

The problem is that this approach—which results in what is commonly called the *essay*—presumes that a writer begin with a clearly defined thesis (a descriptive thesis, an example thesis, a comparison/contrast thesis, a classification thesis, a causal thesis) when in reality many writers write successful expositions that are nothing like an essay. Further in Carolyn Anthony's *Family Portraits* we see many examples of successful family writers who organize expositions around central ideas that would not qualify as expository theses and which are clearly not essays. Consider the following non-thesis, non-essay, organizational approaches:

The Force Of Chronological Details: The Past Leading Into the Present

Daniel J. Boorstin's "My Father: Lawyer Sam Boorstin" is an example of writing in which the details organized chronologically do not prove anything specific about the subject, Sam Boorstin. Each paragraph or section composed of several paragraphs simply adds information about the subject: an introductory paragraph in which the author delineates the relationship between his father and his mother, then paragraphs on his father's immigrant origins, his father's marriage, his father's preference for Tulsa, and his father's law practice. In his conclusion, Boorstin eulogizes his father's tolerance even for Klan bigots and Nazis. But if the reader expects the details of the exposition to prove, persuade, or convince, he will be disappointed. The details of Boorstin's father's life coupled with the organizing force of chronology are all that hold the brief exposition together.

No student need do more than this. If a writer of Boorstin's stature can get away with it, there is absolutely no reason why the beginning student cannot. The only rules are that you organize the paragraphs or sections of paragraphs around some minor idea such as immigrant origins, marriage, or employment, proceed in chronological order from idea to idea, and present only details that deal with the subject of the exposition.

Exercise 2-11

Try developing a similar chronological organizing idea. Pick a subject such as a close relative or friend and briefly jot down the essence of each paragraph you would use to present this subject; arrange the series of supporting items chronologically.

SUBJECT:

DETAILS ARRANGED CHRONOLOGICALLY

Item 1: _____

Item 2: _____

Item 3 _____

Item 4: _____

Item 5: _____

Item 6: _____

The Laying-on-of-hands: The Present as a Fulfillment of the Past

David Bradley in his "Harvest Home" begins with a description of a family gathering at Thanksgiving, but he quickly turns to a generational history: the first generation, Peter the slave; the second generation, Daniel Francis, the minister; and the third generation, the author's. He then returns to Thanksgiving clan gatherings down through the years and shows the impact his Uncle John had on him and how he acquired his uncle's talent for telling tall tales. He closes with the death of Uncle John.

The author sees his life as a product of the values and aspirations of his family, particularly his Uncle John. Again there is no clear thesis unless one insists that he is out to prove or establish that he, the author, is a true product of his family. He simply adds anecdote to anecdote to show how he was touched and molded by his family.

Exercise 2-12

Try developing a similar organizing idea. Isolate three or four generations in your family history, and briefly jot down the essence of each generation. Then present the details of your life story relating the details of your life to the generational history.

Generation 1: _____

_____

Generation 2: _____

_____

Generation 3: _____

_____

Generation 4: _____

_____

DETAILS FROM YOUR LIFE

Item 1: _____

Item 2 _____

Item 3: _____

Item 4: _____

Item 5: _____

Item 6: _____

The Logic Of Emotion: Memories Lead to Other Memories

Joyce Carol Oates' "Facts, Visions, Mysteries: My Father Frederic Oates" is almost a dream reverie, a meditation. One memory triggers another memory, the logic is that of emotion. Her exposition begins with her listening to her father playing the piano. She wonders how this man who had such a "malnourished" upbringing blossomed. She remembers the ugliness of his childhood, then the farm her parents lived on. This reminds her of how she has used her parents' world in her writing which makes her wonder how memory works. She then remembers how her father's memory and hers differ on details of the past. She moves on to a memory of her father flying her in a small airplane. Her discussion of his "avocational" life reminds her of his vocational life, which moves her now back into the present—her father playing the piano.

One emotion, not idea or thesis, triggers another emotion, and the author moves effortlessly from memory to memory. She begins in a dream, moves from emotion to emotion almost in a dream-like state, and returns to her original dream, but the organizing idea is really logic of emotion.

Exercise 2-13

Try developing a similar memory-based organizing idea. Begin with a particular subject—a person or place. Isolate a memory about that person or place. When this memory gives rise to another memory or as the second memory occurs to you, jot down the essence of that memory. Continue as long as you wish.

SUBJECT:

Memory 1: _____

_____

Memory 2: _____

_____

Memory 3: _____

_____

Memory 4: _____

_____

Memory 5: _____

_____

Memory 6: _____

_____

Memory 7: _____

_____

Memory 8: _____

_____

Memory 9: _____

_____

Memory 10: _____

_____

Recalling a Place: Visiting the Past

Elizabeth Spencer in her "Revisiting Teoc" writes what most of us can only dream about. In her mind, she returns home. She describes the family plantation, her uncle and aunt, driving to the plantation as a child, the relationship between the blacks on the plantation and her uncle, her uncle's influence on her reading tastes, her uncle's period of depression when her aunt died, and his death.

The only binding idea of the entire exposition is her recall of the people and places she knew and which were associated with the family plantation. If she remembers it and if it was large enough in her mind, she awards it a place in her description.

Exercise 2-14

Try developing a similar organizing idea based on place. Pick a place that you knew well. Jot down briefly the memories, persons, and events associated with that place:

PLACE:

ASSOCIATED MEMORIES, PERSONS, AND EVENTS

Item 1: _____

Item 2: _____

Item 3: _____

Item 4: _____

Item 5: _____

Item 6: _____

Considering an Artifact: Triggering the Memory with a Physical Object.
Susan Allen Troth and Jonathan Yardley both build their expositions around artifacts, the former around a "worn black briefcase" and the latter around books. Troth begins with a family picture but quickly moves to her father's briefcase, asking what kind of an influence or emotional legacy her father left her. She breaks her answer down into two categories—specifically, fear, and generally, "odds-and-ends" memories—and provides anecdotal examples. Yardley begins his exposition with a reference to the relationship between books and his parents: their courtship and his father's Trollope collection. He then turns to his mother, the real subject of his exposition: his mother's shyness and her love of books, his parents' courtship and books, his mother's rearing of children and her native intelligence, his mother's escape in books, and her death and her last reading.

Exercise 2-15

Try developing a similar organizing idea. Thinking about a person, select an artifact from that person's past. Jot down briefly the various ideas that relate that individual to the artifact.

PERSON:

ASSOCIATED ARTIFACT:

HOW THE INDIVIDUAL AND THE ARTIFACT ARE RELATED

Item 1: _____

Item 2: _____

Item 3: _____

Item 4: _____

Item 5: _____

Item 6: _____

There are as many ways to write an exposition as there are authors. Once again, read widely, observe what others do, and glean techniques that you particularly like and with which you feel comfortable. All this brings us to the next step, sketching a rough outline.

STEP FOUR: SKETCH A ROUGH OUTLINE

Actually we have already begun considering this step. In completing the exercises for the various organizing ideas that we considered at the end of step 2, we would actually be developing rough outlines. The outline of the standard expository essay, however, might look something as follows:

> Thesis: Ted is authoritarian.
>
> 1. Ted expects absolute obedience.
>
> 2. Ted refuses to allow anyone to make decisions.
>
> 3. Ted gives unquestioning obedience to his superiors.
>
> Conclusion: Ted is so authoritarian that living with him is difficult.

The thesis will appear normally as the last sentence in the opening paragraph; each supporting topic sentence will appear at the beginning of each succeeding support paragraph; and finally, the summary statement, which is a restatement of the thesis, will appear in the concluding paragraph. Let us assume that you want to establish that a certain person named Ted will accept no advice in deciding a course of action, in other words that Ted is authoritarian. While the subject of the exposition is Ted, the writer will provide details that deal only with establishing Ted's authoritarian nature.

From the outline, it is clear why points 1, 2, and 3 relate to the thesis and the conclusion. What is probably not immediately evident is how the writer proposes to establish points I, II, and III. Actually any of the above writing strategies would work. The outline could show how Ted has changed from an authoritarian to a more consultative personality:

> Thesis: Ted has changed from an authoritarian to a dependent personality.
>
> 1. Early in his marriage Ted was very authoritarian.
>
> 2. When he married and as he encountered personal problems, he began to turn to others for support.
>
> 3. With the death of his wife and the ensuing years of loneliness, he became completely dependent on his children for direction.

The outline could demonstrate how Ted's authoritarian patterns can be divided into three parts:

> Thesis: Ted's authoritarian personality is seen in three ways.
>
> 1. He demands strict compliance from his children.
>
> 2. He will accept no advice from his wife.
>
> 3. He demands absolute obedience from his subordinates at work.

The outline could show how Ted is similar to his father:

Thesis: Ted is very much like his father.

1. Ted and his father have similar personalities.

2. Ted and his father resemble one another physically.

3. Ted and his father have similar employment.

Or the outline could show what caused him to become authoritarian:

Thesis: There are three things that have caused Ted to become authoritarian.

1. His parents demanded strict obedience of Ted.

2. Ted's training in the U.S. Army developed his authoritarian attitudes.

3. Ted's current employment as a policeman has contributed to his authoritarianism.

STEP FIVE: USING EFFECTIVE DETAIL, WRITE THE EXPOSITION

You are now prepared to begin writing the exposition. As an example, I will explain how I wrote an exposition based on the preliminary work I had done on the Dauer family.

First, working from my pedigree chart, I limited my subject to three centuries of a certain line from my family history. I next chose how I wanted to organize my ideas. I decided on an example expository essay. I then constructed a thesis that adequately explained the total time period. Finally, I wrote a rough outline.

Limited subject: The Dauers of Lauterbourg

Thesis: The Dauers and associated families were survivors.

1. They survived intense instability of the 1600s.

2. They prospered through the tranquility of the 1700s.

3. They survived the political instability and famines of the 1800s by leaving France for the New World.

The key word in my thesis, the so-called controlling idea, is "survivors." Now I turn my attention to fleshing out the outline with effective detail. An effective detail is any specific or detailed supporting statement that establishes the idea of "survivors." I do not repeat over and over again, no matter how clever my restatement of the thesis, that these people were survivors; the repetition of an abstract idea is both boring and pointless. I instead seek to establish the thesis through the specific details of each support example.

To include the entire essay here, in this workbook, is unnecessary; therefore, the example below begins with an opening paragraph, skips over both parts 1 and 2 of the outline, develops part 3 by providing sufficient details to establish the subpoint of part 3, and ends with a conclusion.

The Dauers of Lauterbourg

(Note: *The beginning of the first paragraph is attention-getting. A series of transitional sentences then lead naturally to the thesis, indicated in boldface.*)

When you stop to think about it, the pedigree chart is a rather ridiculous misreading of the past. It presumes that several families somehow concentrated their total efforts in the development of a single family line that led to a single individual, you. However, since I am writing this history largely for myself and for my immediate family, it is perfectly legitimate that I make some arbitrary decisions. Joseph Antoine Waller from Mothern, a small village near Lauterbourg, met and married Magdalena Dauer from Lauterbourg sometime in the early 1830s and briefly thereafter immigrated with her to New York. When I began researching this line, the Waller name in my mind took genealogical precedence over the maternal line, the Dauers, largely because this was the name that came to America and which I, after years of frustrating research, was able to link with Alsace. However, information on the Wallers in France turned out to be meager, and I was only able to trace back into history by abandoning the Waller line and following the Dauer line. The Dauer family of Lauterbourg, Alsace, France, then, emerged naturally as the focus of the several individuals and families that historical accident brought together in Lauterbourg, a small German-speaking corner of France, and to America in the early 1800s. The recorded history of the Dauers began in a period of relative tranquility and growing prosperity, and shifted to America during a period of political instability and economic disaster. **Throughout their entire recorded history, the Dauers and associated families exhibited a keen capacity for survival.**

CENTURY OF TURMOIL: THE 1600s

(Note: *This deleted section focuses on the trauma and devastation of the Thirty Years War, the economic uncertainty that the Dauers and related families experienced, the French pillaging of Alsace, and the migrations of the Dauers and related families seeking economic stability in Alsace; the point is that the Dauers literally by the "skin of their teeth" survived this century of turmoil.*)

CENTURY OF CHANGE: TRANQUILITY AND POLITICAL STABILITY: THE 1700s

(Note: *This deleted section focuses on the developing Alsatian textile industry and the part the Dauers and related families played as artisans; once again the point is that the Dauers prospered, survived well, during this period of tranquility and political stability.*)

PERIOD OF ABANDONMENT: FROM THE FRENCH REVOLUTION TO EMIGRATION

(Note: *In this section, the purpose is to establish that the Dauers and related families survived during the difficult period following the French Revolution by leaving Alsace for the New World.)*

Joseph Antoine Waller and his wife Magdalena Dauer were not able to leave Alsace before the real tragedies occurred; indeed, it was because of these very tragedies that they left. As soon as the terror of the French Revolution and the exhilaration of the Napoleonic era had passed, Alsace had several years of abundance (1818-1827) which were followed by a period of relative penury. Then in 1828, there was a very bad harvest which led to an increase in the price of grain. From 1828 to 1847 there followed a series of crises: 1828-1838 and 1845-1847. After 1848, agricultural shortages and scarcities persisted up to 1855. After 1855, there were nine years of relative abundance.[1] However, it was precisely at the end of the most serious period of agricultural crisis and shortly before matters turned for the better that Joseph Antoine Waller and his wife Magdalena Dauer left Alsace, 1832 or 1833.

Joseph Antoine Waller was born and reared in Mothern which lies about six miles south of Lauterbourg, Magdelana Dauer's place of birth. Today Lauterbourg, although a small city, is considerably larger than Mothern. In 1785, a century after the rampant destruction and loss of life of the 1600s, Lauterbourg and Mothern were the same size, each with approximately 1,200 souls.[2] Even then, though, Lauterbourg was a city that afforded opportunities for a young unemployed laborer that were impossible in Mothern: a weapons workshop, eight breweries, one copper and iron foundry, a potash and salt "fabrique," two tobacco "fabriques," a dye workshop, four tile and brick "fabriques."[3] Probably, it was the opportunity for work that brought Joseph Antoine the some six miles from Mothern; or maybe it was Magdalena Dauer whom he had decided to court. Today, Lauterbourg's central district is hardly impressive, but there are several shops that line both sides of the main street which rises slightly towards the true center of town, the *mairie*, or town hall. Some 150 years ago when Joseph Antoine came to town, though, Lauterbourg shops and busy factories provided real opportunities unknown in Mothern.

Up the hill from Lauterbourg's *mairie* lies a small square in front of the town's main church. It was probably here, then, that my ancestors, the Dauers, had come to be christened, married, and buried. And it was probably from here in 1832 or 33 that a young Magdalena Dauer of Lauterbourg and Joseph Antoine Waller in company with Joseph's brother Bernhard of Mothern had taken leave of the Dauers never again to lay eyes on the beautiful Alsatian plains, the impoverished villages, and the mountains closing out on the east and on the west the vast hostile world that so periodically rained down terror. Joseph Antoine and Magdalena had met probably in Lauterbourg and walked several times along that lovely road between Mothern and Lauterbourg, marrying according to family tradition in the Old Country before coming to the United States. And it was probably from here, accompanied by Joseph Antoine and Bernhard Waller's sisters and mother and Magdalena Dauer's parents and friends, that they carried a few

1 Lerch, op cit., 307.
2 Dictionnaire geographique, historique et politique de l'Alsace, Tome Premier. Strasbourg: L'Imprimerie de Levrault, 1787, 65 and 70.
3 Renseignements Statistiques sur plusieurs objects importants de l'administration du Bas-Rhin, adresses au Ministre de lInterieur, par le Prefet dudit Department. (See Orion at UCLA for better citation, DC 611 B28 L3.)

belongings down to the Rhine River to board a flat-bottomed boat for the lowlands of Holland—and then out across the open sea for the uncertainties of the New World.

In 1853, approximately twenty years after Joseph and his wife Magdalena had left Alsace, Joseph's sisters wrote two letters to Joseph who was at that time residing in Manitowoc, Wisconsin, on the shores of Lake Michigan. They had tried on three previous occasions—initially on the death of his mother in May of 1849—to contact Joseph and his brother Bernard who was at the time residing in Cincinnati, but not one of those letters reached either brother. Eventually Joseph heard through friends of his mother's death and a lost inheritance, concluded that his brothers-in-law and sisters had conspired to cheat him and his brother, and wrote demanding an explanation.

A few years ago, I visited Mothern, Alsace, France, the village next to Lauterbourg and from which Joseph Antoine Waller left in the 1830s. Today it is an obscure but beautiful village of approximately 1,700 persons, situated along the Rhine approximately six miles south of the town of Lauterbourg which itself lies at the northeast corner of France. Leaving behind the admixture of new and ancient half-timbered houses of Mothern, I drove my rented Volkswagen along the road to Lauterbourg, skirting a cliff and then a wood that separated my view from the river. This valley, formed geological eons ago by the meanderings of the Rhine that had served for centuries as one of the main social and economic arteries of Europe and carried thousands of refugees into and out of the broad war-torn plain, formed a peculiar and suspended beauty which seemed almost to deny its historical significance. To the left of the road and in the distance rose the Vosges Mountains of France, quaintly wild and picturesque at the same time; and to the right across the river lay first the plains of Baden-Wuertenberg and then the mystic hills of the Black Forest of Germany. The Rhine cuts this peaceful plain into two worlds, France (Alsace or Bas-Rhin) and Germany (Baden-Wuertenberg) and although linguistically and culturally it is more German than French, centuries of political chaos and intense social pain have left Alsace psychically scarred and nationalistically ambivalent.

When I visited Alsace in the spring, nature had given this corner of France a misleading and suspended tranquility. It was difficult to visualize the poverty and natural calamity that made the mid-nineteenth century a time of disease, famine, depression, and emigration. In 1853, blight, hail, high winds, and humidity had destroyed vast areas planted in wheat near Colmar (a town south of Mothern); a few short years later drought destroyed entire sections of potatoes.

> En 1853, un deficit de la production agricole est encoure signale, les causes sont une temperature excessivement douce en automne et en hiver et qui a developpe la vegetation outre mesure, des froids tardifs au printemps, les pluies qui se sont succede soit a la flouraison, soit a l'epoque de l'eqiage et de la maturation, sont les causes primitives des maladies . . . [4]

The period of suffering had begun in 1828 and was to end in 1855, but the three surviving daughters of Johannes Waller and Eva Catharina Stupfel had no way of knowing in 1853

---

4   Dominique Lerch, "Le paysan haut-rhinois au XIXe siecle: contribution a une histoire des mentalities en Alsace, " *Histoire de l'Alsace rurale* (Strasbourg: Libraire Istra, 1983, 305-306.)

that the crisis would last only two more years; and even if they had known, they would have probably done little else except to endure whatever God was to send their way. Johannes and Eva Catharina Waller had had five daughters, but only three had survived to maturity: Anne Maria who married Bernard Rueck, Magdalena who married Johann Michael Meyer, and Marguerithe. They had had three sons: Johann, who died when he was sixteen, and Joseph Antoine and Bernhard who both left Alsace. The surviving sisters had remained in Alsace to begin families while the surviving brothers left to begin life anew in America.

When Johannes Waller, the father, had died in 1826 at the early age of fifty, the sons were still at home. But when in 1849 Eva Catharina, the mother, at the age of sixty-eight died, the two surviving brothers had been living in the United States for a decade. And communication was difficult. Bernhard had kept in contact by sending greetings via some mutual friends when he lived in Cincinnati, Ohio. But when their mother died, it took four more years for Joseph Antoine to learn of her death. The sisters had tried three times to reach Joseph Antoine. One letter they had sent registered, and two letters they themselves had taken to the post; but none had reached him. Fourteen years is a long time, and in the 1850s America was a very long way from Alsace, France; but somehow, Joseph Antoine learned of his mother's death, and forgotten relationships and obligations once again became very important. On 29 July 1853, he wrote a scathing letter accusing his sisters and their husbands of duplicity. Why had they not tried to reach him? Were they keeping him deliberately in the dark about her death so that they could inherit alone the family property?

And so on 14 August of 1853, the three sisters with their husbands sat down to write a letter which has survived to this day. The stamp has three postmarks: Wissembourg, Paris, and Le Havre, and the letter is addressed to Mr. Joseph Antoine Waller of Manitowoc City in North America. No wonder the other letters had not survived. It is amazing that this one managed to arrive. The letter is a plea for understanding and trust. After fourteen years, they still thought and worried about him. They wanted him to offer one son to God, presumably as a priest. They pleaded that he understand that they had not deceived and cheated him, that either an Englishman or more likely someone named Englaender had brought civil action against them in court for an old debt contracted by their mother, and this had apparently tied up the inheritance. They continued that their mother had never been anything but just and that they had also been just. But their letter reveals the harsh world Joseph Antoine and his brother Bernard had left behind:

> Beloved brother, here at home everything is a large famine; you thresh
> a half a "sester" from nine sheaves, and the potatoes are rotting. It has
> been nine years since we had a good year, but still we managed to have
> fruit, but this year everything has turned to mildew and has hardly
> grown.

And then on 14 December 1853, they wrote in a second letter that they had received Joseph's "Vollmacht" or authority and that they had forwarded 803 francs, presumably Joseph Antoine's portion of the estate. The financial and legal matters were apparently settled, but conditions in Alsace were serious and difficult. But Joseph Antoine Waller had somehow escaped, and now flushed with his inheritance of 803 francs, Joseph Antoine and his Magdalena began to acquire property in the New World. Out of the penury and poverty of the Old World, the Dauers and related families would survive and even prosper in the New.

CONCLUSION

(Note: *Now restating my thesis, in bold, I proceed to conclude the entire essay, ending my conclusions with a send-off, a reminder that we owe our sense of survival to our European heritage.*)

When there was stability in the land, the Dauers and related families took advantage of that stability both in their remaining close to Latuerbourg and to one another and in following primarily artisan occupations that depended on a stable and growing economy. When there was uncertainty and political turmoil, they scratched the earth, moved where opportunity beckoned, and whether in the seventeenth or in the nineteenth century broke and reestablished personal and familial ties as events required it of them. **These people, common and very ordinary, were linked together in one great aspiration: survival.** What is most fascinating, though, is that the quality of endurance and the instinct for survival that we normally associate with the American pioneer, the quality and instinct that we feel made America great, was part of the Dauers long before they came to America, indeed long before many of them had even arrived in France from other parts of Europe. The Dauers teach us that as Americans we should recognize the gift that Europe gave us and understand that Europe bequeathed to us that which made them great. Above all else, the Dauers show us that we are truly sons of the Old World.

Up to this point, I have developed only an introductory history. Obviously, there is much to do, but the principle remains the same: limit the subject, develop a thesis, write a rough outline, and use specific details to bring alive the main points of the exposition.

SOME FINAL COMMENTS

As we use genealogical and local history sources, we accumulate facts for which there is no place on the standard genealogical pedigree or family group sheet. The tragedy is that most genealogists and family researchers feel that their task is complete when they have finished filling out the charts and group sheets, viewing the miscellaneous notes as fascinating but incidental addenda to the real task of pushing the family back into time, promptly filing and forgetting these vital notes.

No single task, however, is so important to completing and finalizing the whole business of "doing genealogy" as that of writing. Why? Because gathering and recording disjointed facts is actually only one step removed from leaving them ungathered in dusty manuscripts and on microfilm reels. The essence of genealogical and family history research is not the facts themselves but what those facts mean. The first obstacle that the amateur family researcher faces is learning how to locate information about his family. With childlike enthusiasm, he joins organizations, attends endless meetings, and enrolls in classes filled with overbearing genealogical successes; all too often he loses interest and falls by the wayside. That persistent and elected body of true believers who do find their family names in federal or state censuses or in a probate document, find the next obstacle insurmountable. Having located, recorded, and filed reams of material, most genealogists or family historians mentally dump all those precious facts into files and mercifully forget exactly what it was they have found, let alone how one fact or set of facts relate to others. The armies of amateur researchers who meticulously enter countless and historically isolated facts into pedigree charts and family group sheets are like flocks of vultures who pick all the human and emotional flesh off the skeletal remains of the past, leaving only the whitened remains of historical personalities to litter the familial landscape. There is, however, a way to interpret and correlate or to synthesize genealogical facts: it is through the writing process that we evaluate what facts mean and have meant in their social and historical context, that we see relationships between disjointed items, and that we build meaningful portraits of historical events and human beings.

The section in *WFN* chapter 2 entitled "From Thesis to History: the Techniques of Exposition" (48–59) is one important step in the writing process. For many, it is the only step, most electing never to write a family narrative. There is absolutely nothing wrong with this approach. But before one can write a family narrative, one must be adept at gathering facts and writing historical exposition. If not, the family narrative becomes an exercise in fantasy.

CHAPTER 3

SHAPING CHARACTERS AND PLOT

WRITING THE NARRATIVE

The distinction between exposition and narrative is both easy and difficult to understand. Exposition is a piece of writing that explains, establishes, and proves a thesis, an assertion with a controlling idea. A narrative is a story. However, a narrative can also explain, establish, or prove a main point which, while technically not a thesis, is still a central idea. In *WFN* chapter 2, we considered techniques of exposition and focused on three types: description, example, and process. We also touched on classification, causal analysis, and comparison/contrast. It is easier to understand exactly what exposition is, not by elaborating on abstract definitions but by seeing examples of what it is (for more examples of this technique, refer back to chapter 2). The narrator may well make a point, technically even establish a thesis, but instead of organizing the body of his paper with a series of examples or contrasts, he makes his point by telling a story or a series of stories. And here, description becomes vital. The better the narrator can describe his characters or show those characters in a plot, the better the story. The purpose of the following exercises is to help the narrator develop both his characters and his plots.

I presume that you have read the second chapters of both *WFN and Workbook* carefully and, after understanding the prewriting techniques as they apply to exposition, have kept a family historian's notebook by gathering quotes, responding to what others have written, listing topics, recording clustering and brainstorming activities, and writing freely with the purpose in mind of eventually developing an historical exposition. Now you want to transform some or part of your exposition into a narrative. Therefore, when I make references to prewriting activities as they apply to the narrative, I will assume that you are already familiar with these activities explained previously. While many family historians are very uneasy about writing a narrative, as we proceed it will become clear that the techniques of narrative are simply the techniques of telling a story well, an approach that even the most factually oriented historian can hardly gainsay. Indeed both forms of writing lend themselves to one another, and the writer who refuses to venture into the domain of the narrative limits his effectiveness as a family historian.

STEP ONE: CHARACTERIZATION

The important beginning considerations for the writer of the narrative are the three methods of character presentation: characterization through direct or explicit exposition; characterization through thoughts and dialogue; and characterization through action *(WFN 81-96)*. In other t words, we have three basic ways in which we normally gather and impart information about a character: through a description of the character, through a presentation of the thoughts and dialogue of the character, and through a recitation of the actions of the character. This presumes an important basic skill: knowing how to observe characters so well that we can clearly and without confusion make those characters understandable as well as believable to the reader. Luckily for the beginner, psychology has made character analysis as well as character description a matter of study. However, while psychology has added immeasurably to our basic understanding of human nature, we must be careful not to fall into the trap of allowing "pop" psychology or any other academic discipline to underlie our descriptions. Most readers simply are not interested in character descriptions developed out of transactional analysis or the technical jargon of the Meyers-Briggs Personality Inventory. The key is learning how to observe without betraying the mode of analysis and to impart that observation in a natural and straightforward manner. For the family historian or writer of the family narrative, the problem is not so much observing as consulting and analyzing sources that will reveal the details needed to write the characterization.

Exercise 3-1

First, make a list of the sources you might be able to use to write a characterization. The following is a beginning list of the different types of sources available:

military records	inventories	employment records
city maps	pictures	school annals
letters	journals	obituaries
oral interviews and histories	family traditi	onsinsurance maps
newspapers	plat maps	county histories

Now add your sources:

_____

_____

_____

_____

_____

_____

_____

Second, gather the details. Learning how to describe a character is as simple as learning how to be specific in noting what you observe about a person. Observe someone, preferably someone in your family, or consult the sources you have before you; make notations in your notebook about the following items:

DETAILS OF GENERAL SETTING

Geographic location: _____

Common occupations and daily manner of living: _____

_____

Time or period: _____

CHARACTER'S PHYSICAL DESCRIPTION

Age (young, mature, old) or birthday: _____

Race: _____

Sex: _____

Height: _____

Build (thin, medium, heavy): _____

State of health: _____

Posture (normal, slumped, rigid): _____

Clothes (neat, untidy): _____

Posture: _____

CHARACTER'S PERSONAL BACKGROUND (MENTAL, MORAL, SOCIAL, AND EMOTIONAL)

Education: _____

_____

_____

Occupation: *PN keeping house for brother*
LP student

Quality of work: _____

Military service: *N/A*

Family

Father's profession: *PN farmer d 1853*
LP

Parents' marriage: _____

Siblings: *LP none*

Family values: _____

Talents: _____

CHARACTER'S THOUGHTS AND DIALOGUE

Speech

Languages spoken: _Engl_____

Speed (slow, normal, or rapid): _____

Volume (soft, normal, loud): _____

Amount (muted, normal, verbose): _____

Behavior

Bearing (friendly, evasive, arrogant, hostile, cooperative):_____

_____

_____

Mood (fearful, depressed):_____

_____

_____

Fears: _____

_____

_____

Complexes:_____

_____

_____

Personal values: _____

_____

_____

Attitudes about different things: _____

_____

_____

Frustrations: _____

_____

_____

Slang and idioms he often uses: _____

_____

_____

Feelings he often has: _____

_____

_____

What does he say when he is angry? _____

_____

_____

What does he say when he is happy? _____

_____

_____

CHARACTER'S SIGNIFICANT ACTIONS

Typical mannerisms: _____

_____

_____

_____

Dreams and ambitions: _____

_____

_____

_____

What he finds fun: _____

_____

_____

_____

Things he normally does: _____

_____

_____

_____

Things he hates to do: _____

_____

_____

_____

The disagreements he has with people: _____

_____

_____

_____

How does he handle stress? _____

_____

_____

_____

How does he solve problems? _____

_____

_____

_____

How does he relate to people? _____

_____

_____

_____

What is the happiest/saddest thing that ever happened to him?

_____

_____

_____

What has been the hardest experience of his life?

_____

_____

_____

_____

Develop a Character Generalization

ISOLATE PRIMARY AND SECONDARY CHARACTER QUALITIES

Now that you have recorded what you have observed, consider carefully the items noted and draw a conclusion or make a generalization about this person. This conclusion can be one word or a simple phrase; essentially, this would be a dominant or primary quality. Above all else, do not fall into the trap of making a generalized moral evaluation. We are writing a characterization, not a spiritual report card. Too many people feel obligated to describe someone close to them as "good," "honest," "loving," or "devoted." While these qualities may all be accurate and certainly no one would argue that there are people who have these traits as dominant qualities, moral evaluations are often both too general to be workable and too much of a smokescreen to allow us to see the reality of a person's character. Isolate a dominant and specific trait such as "determined," "long-suffering," "sensitive," "ambitious," "dour," "vain," "stubborn," "judgmental," "emotional," "quick," "calculating," or "manipulating." Any person who is determined and/or stubborn can as well be loving and devoted, but the terms "determined" and "stubborn" are more specific and thus easier to work with than the far more general term "loving." Note under this one term the synonyms (consult a thesaurus) that express the same idea. Now consider actual things that this person did or does (not synonyms) that are in your mind associated with or are examples of this dominant quality. Think of ways in which this character has exhibited the quality of being a "disciplined" person: he is often prompt in paying his bills, orderly in solving problems and meeting a crisis, neat in placing his socks and other personal items in his chest of drawers, and responsible in completing little jobs around the house that his spouse brings to his attention. In other words, although "prompt," "orderly," "neat," and "responsible" are qualities related to discipline, each associated or related quality is not listed as an isolated term but linked with a specific personality pattern. And this is vitally important because "neat" in isolation is never as helpful in writing an effective characterization as telling specifically how the character was neat (e.g., neat in placing his socks and other personal items in his chest of drawers). So as you list related qualities, be careful to link each quality with specific actions that demonstrate this quality.

Exercise 3-2

PRIMARY CHARACTER QUALITY:

List synonyms: _____

_____

_____

_____

_____

_____

_____

_____

Associated or related qualities and actions that demonstrate this quality: _____

_____

_____

_____

_____

_____

_____

_____

WRITE A CHARACTERIZATION

Now that you have a dominant trait in mind, and you have three or four associated or related qualities linked with some specific personality pattern, consider various ways to present your character.

Describe Him, His Physical Makeup, His Clothes.

> The Nilsa family had tilled and lived on this farm as far back in history as paper is preserved, as far as memory of generations can reach. The first known owner was Nils in Mjödahult after whom the family got its name. About Nils in Mjödahult it is further known that he had an unusually large and grotesque nose, which was said to have resembled a well-grown rutabaga. This nose was inherited by his descendants, and someone in each generation possessed it. It became a mark of the Nilsa family. Called the Nilsa-nose, it was believed to be endowed with the same magic powers as a birth cowl, and brought luck to its owner. Children born with the Nilsa-nose became the most fortunate and most successful members of the family, and, even though it was hardly a mark of beauty in a woman, it is not known to have been an obstacle in securing advantageous marriages.

> — Moberg, *The Emigrants*

Exercise 3-3

Referring to the lists you prepared in exercise 3-2, present your character by describing him:

_____

_____

_____

_____

_____

_____

_____

Present Him Through His Environment, His House, His Town, His Era.

> One could approach the Village, as it was called in 1819, by a ride of a few miles, mostly westward from Boston. Founded in 1632 by Governor John Winthrop as a self-govern-

ing town, Cambridge was settled now on the banks of the Charles, a stable community of five thousand well-rested souls. Traveling the rising countryside by way of the New Road, one might pause on the brow of Symond's Hill to take in the distant view. In the foreground stretched the town itself, tufted with the foliage of elms, lindens, and horse chestnuts, above which rose the noisy belfry of the landmark college, the square brown tower of the church, the thin yellow spire of the parish meetinghouse. To the left on the Old Road stood some half-dozen dignified houses of colonial vintage, all comfortably fronting southward. On the fight, the broad and serpentine fiver glided through green and purple salt meadows, darkened at intervals with blossoming black grass. Beyond the marshes that surrounded it, low hills defined a gray horizon.

— Heymann, *American Aristocracy*

Exercise 3-4

Present your character in his environment:

_____

_____

_____

_____

_____

_____

_____

_____

See him as part of his personal background: his family, his talents, his education.

Such was the environment into which I was born.

I have said nothing yet of my mother's family, from which I get all my inherited characteristics, temperament, emotional disposition, and so on. If I get anything from the Rowses (I do not take after them physically) it is only a certain pugnacity, for they were excessively pugnacious, impatience, shortness of temper, a gift for music: a deep love of it which, had it been given a chance, might have determined my life for me in quite a different direction, for nothing carries me away as music does—not poetry, not painting, nor religion, nor politics (that is on an altogether lower level: the public, as opposed to the private, life), not even love or friendship, nothing. I think I would rather have been a great musician, or just a pianist, than anything, as certainly it is the life and works of a great composer, a Beethoven or Bach, Mozart or Schubert, a Brahms or Debussy--but, most of all, Beethoven--that I admire above all human kind. In default, perhaps, of that, there is something frustrated about my life and its modes of self-expression. I have thought sometimes that it was for want of the religious life:

> opening the casements
> upon what inner kingdoms,
> what peace forgotten,
> save in the unquiet tongues of bells
> ringing to church on Christmas Eve...

as I have written in my poem in memory of Charles Henderson. Even there it is to be noticed that the mood is induced by the sound of bells ringing, for with me music and religion are inseparably entwined. But I know which is fundamental.

There could hardly be a greater contrast than between my father's family and my mother's. The Rowses were a family of men, the Vansons were mainly women; and certainly where masculine traits almost exclusively characterized the one, in the other the feminine element was markedly dominant (even in the men, I think). There was a regular Rowse physical type: short, thickset, muscular, energetic, inclining to be stout, round-headed, and many of them--Bill, my father, Harry, Edwin--were sandy-haired and blue-eyed. My mother's family were all tall, long-headed and dark.' Mediterranean type (Atlantic extension), and I should add they were distinctly good-looking, which the Rowses were not. In character there was as great a contrast; where the one was fiery, fighting and rather dare-devil, miners' stock, the other was passive, well-mannered, emotional, cautious, inclined to make its way by distinct strain of obsequiousness and flattery. In short, it looks very much like my contrast between the men of the 'Higher Quarter' and those of the coastal plain, the miners as opposed to the men on the arable land.

— A.L. Rowse, *A Cornish Childhood*

Exercise 3-5

Now present your character as part of his personal background, his family, his talents, his education:

_____

_____

_____

_____

_____

_____

_____

_____

_____

Show him in action.

At lunch in a crowded, cramped restaurant, he had dug his spoon into a grapefruit and a drop shot off onto the neck of a woman at the next table. Just thinking of it, he laughed so that his shoulders bounced and his face collapses. He had twisted the grapefruit around to go after another section, and this time he hit the woman in the ear. When she turned, he hid the grapefruit behind cupped hands and played innocent. Then he decided he would try to control his shot, and just as the stream left the fruit the woman turned again and caught the juice right above the eye.

He had been stuttering and gasping, but he sobered to say, "Of course I would never have tried such a thing, but she was smoking."

— Packer, *In My Father's House*

Exercise 3-6

Now present your character showing him in action, referring to the list you prepared in exercise 3-2.

_____

_____

_____

_____

_____

_____

_____

_____

_____

_____

_____

_____

Let the character reveal himself through his speech.

"How about medicine—do you take any medicine?"

"Never. Oh, sometimes I'll take a Rolaid or something like that when my stomach gets sour, and I've taken a few aspirin, but generally I don't take any medicine. I think I'd have been dead a long time ago if I'd gotten into that."

"Did you ever wear glasses?"

"Yeah, about forty years ago I had a blood clot on my left eye, and when I was being treated for it I discovered that I was very nearsighted in my right eye. I had glasses made and wore them for about a year, but finally I got accustomed to not using them. My eyes don't focus at the same distance, so I just use one for close up and the other for far off. Neither one of them works very well now, but I still manage to read all day, just by holding things up close."

"When was the last time you went to a doctor?"

"I don't remember--it's been six or seven years, I guess."

"Do you have a family doctor?"

"No, I don't. Dr. Kinnaird's dead, Dr. Montgomery's dead—I guess I don't have one. I stopped one time to have my lungs checked at one of those machines on the street, and the nurse asked me who my doctor was, and I told her, 'I ain't got one--they're all dead.'"

— Egerton, "An American Family"

Exercise 3-7

Now present your character revealing himself in his speech (refer to the questions you answered in exercise 3-1).

_____

_____

_____

_____

_____

_____

_____

_____

STEP TWO: PLOT CONFLICT AND THE NARRATIVE

Establishing the Basic Theme

Most of us are very well acquainted with the genealogist who with enthusiasm and emotional fervor comers unsuspecting victims and tells his entire family history without once being aware that the listener is bored beyond tears. What makes such an experience bearable is when the teller touches on a name or a place that reminds us of something from our own family history; and then we are interested. But sometimes we hear a story that has no direct bearing on our family history and still holds our interest. Why? The answer is simply that the story seems to be going somewhere.

With the narrative the author is not attempting as she does in an exposition to show how subpoints support and relate intellectually to one main point for the purpose of proving something. She is telling a story, relating a narrative, the purpose of which is normally to establish and resolve one main problem. One example of this is the autobiography of Beryl Markham, *West with the Night*. Markham focuses ultimately on resolving one basic problem: her solo flight across the Atlantic. While that story takes only a few pages (the second-to-last chapter in the book), Markham builds to the last story with several substories involving the basic conflict of man versus nature. Book 1 deals with her recovery of a downed pilot; book 2 deals with her learning to hunt wild animals with African natives; and book 3 deals with her training of horses. Finally, book 4 brings us to her ultimate challenge of nature--her solo flight across the Atlantic. In an exposition, the writer works within a strict intellectual framework relating details to subideas or topic sentences and the topic sentences to a main thesis and conclusion for the purpose of establishing or convincing the reader of something, while in the narrative the writer basically tells a story of a problem.

In other words, the story that holds our interest has a plot: a problem that is being addressed and resolved. It all begins with a basic problem.

Exercise 3-8

In chapter 3 of *WFN* (97-104) I introduced Polti's thirty-six "dramatic situations" and reduced them to fourteen basic themes. I have listed the fourteen themes below for your convenience. Let your eye run down the list again. Pick out one or several that interest you, and briefly describe in your own words one or several problems from your experience or research that would fit into that theme category.

Dealing with a threat: _____

_____

_____

Taking vengeance or being pursued in vengeance: _____

_____

_____

Overcoming or not overcoming an obstacle: _____

_____

_____

Seizing something or someone: _____

_____

_____

Solving or not solving a problem: _____

_____

_____

Being in a position of rivalry with a relative: _____

_____

_____

Confronting a catastrophic circumstance: _____

_____

_____

Making a sacrifice for an ideal, a relative, or a passion: _____

_____

_____

Competing with a superior individual: _____

_____

_____

Being so much in love that one commits a crime, loves an enemy, or finds one's love dishonored or thwarted: _____

_____

_____

Being confronted with an obstacle to one's personal ambition: _____

_____

_____

Making a terrible mistake that results in pain to someone else: _____

_____

_____

Suffering remorse for a crime: _____

_____

_____

Losing or recovering someone: _____

_____

_____

Inherent to the concept of problem or barrier is the idea of conflict. One cannot or will not achieve his or her goal without overcoming the barrier or resolving the problem, and that places one person in the story, the hero or protagonist, in direct conflict with someone else, himself or a part of his own personality, society at large, or nature. So each problem or barrier is essentially a conflict.

Exercise 3-9

Select a few plot themes that are especially applicable to the narrative you are writing. Then list three specific problems under each plot theme. Note exactly who is in conflict with whom or what.

PLOT THEME:

Problem A: _____

_____

_____

_____ is in conflict with _____

Problem B: _____

_____

_____

_____

_____ is in conflict with _____

Problem C: _____

_____

_____

_____ is in conflict with _____

PLOT THEME:

Problem A: _____

_____

_____

_____ is in conflict with _____

Problem B: _____

_____

_____

_____ is in conflict with _____

Problem C: _____

_____

_____

_____ is in conflict with _____

PLOT THEME:

Problem A: _____

_____

_____

_____ is in conflict with _____

Problem B: _____

_____

_____

_____ is in conflict with _____

Problem C: _____

_____

_____

_____ is in conflict with _____

PLOT THEME:

Problem A: _____

_____

_____

_____ is in conflict with _____

Problem B: _____

_____

_____

_____ is in conflict with _____

Problem C: _____

_____

_____

_____ is in conflict with _____

The idea of conflict causes problems for many amateur family narrators. They feel that conflict is to be avoided in writing family history because to accuse then parents or family of conflict is to somehow open the door on some shameful family skeleton. Conflict, however, does not have to be violent or disruptive and is a normal part of every life. But far more important, conflict brings interest to a narrative.

If a conflict is not natural to the story, however, do not feel that the story will fail. Willa Cather's short story "Neighbour Rosicky" is an excellent example of a description that builds on the contrast between the naturally good Rosicky and the sophisticated physician-narrator, but Cather did not build the story around a conflict. Willa Cather knew the model for "Neighbour Rosicky," and she relied on her keen observational powers to reflect in print what she had seen. Cather begins with Doctor Burleigh's informing Rosicky that he has a bad heart, followed by Burleigh's reflecting on a recent visit to the Rosicky household. Note how detailed, specific, and "artifactual" her description of the kitchen is.

> He had driven in just when the boys had come back from the barn and were washing up for breakfast. The long table, covered with a bright oilcloth, was set out with dishes waiting for them, and the warm kitchen was full of the smell of coffee and hot biscuit and sausage. Five big handsome boys, running from twenty to twelve, all with what Burleigh called natural good manners—they hadn't a bit of the painful self-consciousness he himself had to struggle with when he was a lad. One ran to put his horse away, another helped him off with his fur coat and hung it up, and Josephine, the youngest child and the only daughter, quickly set another place under her mother's direction.

Only someone who had actually eaten in that kitchen could have captured every specific detail that Cather did. The contrast between the two characters--not a conflict--ends the short story.

> The next morning he got up and dressed and sat down to breakfast with his family. He told Mary that his coffee tasted better than usual to him, and he warned the boys not to bear any tales to Doctor Ed when he got home. After breakfast he sat down by his window to do some patching and asked Mary to thread several needles for him before she went to feed her chickens, -- her eyes were better than his, and her hands steadier. He lit his pipe and took up John's overalls. Mary had been watching him anxiously all morning, and as she went out of the door with her bucket of scraps, she saw that he was smiling. He was thinking, indeed, about Polly, and how he might never have known what a tender heart she had if he hadn't got sick over there. Girls nowadays didn't wear their heart on their sleeve. But now he knew Polly would make a Free woman after the foolishness wore off. Either a woman had that sweetness at her heart or she hadn't. You couldn't always tell by the look of them; but if they had that, everything came out right in the end.

> After he had taken a few stitches, the cramp began in his chest, like yesterday. He put his pipe cautiously down on the window-sill and bent over to ease the pull. No use,--he had better try to get to his bed if he could. He rose and groped his way across the familiar floor, which was rising and falling like the deck of a ship. At the door he fell. When Mary came in, she found him lying there, and the moment she touched him she knew that he was gone.

> Doctor Ed was away when Rosicky died, and for the first few weeks after he got home he was hard driven. Every day he said to himself that he must get out to see that family that had lost their father. One soft, warm moonlight night in early summer he started for the farm. His mind was on other things, and not until his road ran by the graveyard did

he realize that Rosicky wasn't over there on the hill where the red lamplight shone, but here, in the moonlight. He stopped his car, shut off the engine, and sat there for a while.

A sudden hush had fallen on his soul. Everything here seemed strangely moving and significant, though signifying what, he did not know. Close by the wire fence stood Rosicky's mowing-machine, where one of the boys had been cutting hay that afternoon; his own work-horses had been going up and down there. The new-cut hay perfumed all the night air. The moonlight silvered the long, billowy grass that grew over the graves and hid the fence; the few little evergreens stood out black in it, like shadows in a pool. The sky was very blue and soft, the stars rather faint because the moon was full.

For the first time it struck Doctor Ed that this was really a beautiful graveyard. He thought of city cemeteries; acres of shrubbery and heavy stone, so arranged and lonely and unlike anything in the living world. Cities of the dead, indeed; cities of the forgotten, of the "put away." But this was open and free, this little square of long grass which the wind forever stirred. Nothing but the sky overhead, and the many-coloured fields running on until they met that sky. The horses worked here summer; the neighbours passed on their way to town; and over yonder, in the cornfield, Rosicky's own cattle would be eating fodder as winter came on. Nothing could be more undeathlike than this place, nothing could be more right for a man who had helped to do the work of great cities and had always longed for the open country and had got to it at last. Rosicky's life seemed to him complete and beautiful.

— Willa Cather, "Neighbour Rosicky"

Building the Scenes of a Plot

Now that we have established the basic theme or problem of our story, the next step is getting there. Basically, getting there is meeting challenges or barriers that increase in intensity and difficulty until we solve our problem. Harold Weston, in his book *Form in Literature,* created what is called the W Diagram, which is basically built on "pivotal points of action."

First, the intent

Second, the barrier

Then, the barrier reversed

High point of action

Second reversal

Then, the catastrophe

Finally, the resolution

If you were to rotate the above set of words ninety degrees counterclockwise, you would see a W, hence the W Diagram.

Other writers see the progression through the plot as increasingly downward until one reaches absolute bottom, then as moving definitely upward to resolution. Rita Oleyar, in "The Job Story," sees Job's movement through the plot as downward until he reaches chapter 17 of the Old Testament, "Where is My Hope?" In chapter 19, he becomes defiant and moves upward towards restoration.

The point is really the same. The hero or heroine has a problem, an adversary which he sets out to overcome. As he proceeds toward the resolution of his problem, he encounters an initial setback in the form of a barrier; and his dogged, innovative, or heroic determination to overcome this reversal brings him to the point of high action, where it would appear that the hero is about to overcome his adversary and resolve the basic problem. At this point, however, he encounters a catastrophe, a second and disastrous barrier that plunges him as it did Job to the very depths of despair, which was reached when Job cried out "Where is My Hope?" Somehow, the hero manages to overcome this catastrophe, emerge from this ultimate form of destruction, and advance towards the resolution of the problem.

Now let us consider a story about a man named Ted. The task is to sketch out the scenes of the story that will develop the resolution of the basic problem of the plot: first, the intent stated; second, the encountering and reversal of the initial barrier; third, the catastrophe; and finally, the emergence of the hero from this near disaster, ultimately resulting in the resolution of the basic problem. One student established the following sequence of events to show how her husband, Ted, overcame a physical adversary, a tunnel:

1. Ted is determined to take the family motor home on a narrow road where signs prohibit motor homes. (intent stated)

2. They come to a second sign that strictly prohibits motor home traffic on the narrow road. (initial barrier)

3. Ted advances through the retreating traffic towards and into the tunnel. (reversal of initial barrier leading to high point of action)

4. With the support of his daughter and onlookers, Ted optimistically continues through the tunnel. (second reversal)

5. Ted drives the motor home slowly into an ever-narrowing tunnel to the point that it would appear that he is wedged between the walls. (catastrophe)

6. Ted presses on to emerge successfully from the other side of the tunnel. (conflict resolved)

While the following story is based on a conflict between the husband and nature, there is the added, interest-raising conflict of the husband with the members of the family. However, the story hangs mainly on the conflict that the husband enters into when he drives the family motor home down a road that leads to a very narrow tunnel.

The Tunnel

Our family has always enjoyed doing things together, and traveling is one of the things we like best. Every summer when the children were younger we would load them into our motor home and start driving. We really put the miles on the odometer in those days and added to the list of states we had visited. It was lots of fun exploring new places.

Twice we traveled for an entire summer, going wherever we wanted whenever we wanted and staying as long as we wished in each place. We avoided the freeways and expressways as much as possible, preferring to travel the backroads that took us through the little towns and past farms and factories. Whenever we saw a sign indicating that something interesting lay ahead of us, we'd make a point of stopping. Sometimes we'd go many miles out of our way to visit a factory, an old battlefield, or an amusement park. We didn't want to miss anything, and we did a pretty thorough job of seeing our country.

Although we've had lots of memorable experiences in our travels, a few incidents stand out as exceptional. Our trip through the Black Hills of South Dakota was one of those experiences none of us will ever forget.

1.   Ted is determined to take the family motor home on a narrow road where signs prohibit motor homes. (intent stated)

As I mentioned before, whenever we saw a sign pointing out something worth seeing, we made every effort to include it in our itinerary. Perhaps that is why when we saw the sign saying "Tunnel Road, Turn Right," we turned right. There was also a sign that said "Narrow Tunnel Ahead. Absolutely No Trucks Or Trailers!" And then there was another sign that said "Absolutely No Trucks Or Trailers Beyond This Point. Low Clearance Ahead." My husband's spirit of adventure is not easily quashed, however, and so we continued up the road in our motor home.

"Dear," I said tactfully, "don't you think we ought to turn around. We've seen lots of tunnels before, and there are lots of other beautiful things to see here in the Black Hills."

"Don't you worry," he said. "We'll make it. We will have lots of room. Just you wait and see."

2.   They come to a second sign that strictly prohibits motor home traffic on the narrow road. (initial barrier)

Another sign loomed ahead. "Very Narrow Tunnel Ahead. Trucks And Trailers Must Turn Around. Do Not Proceed Beyond This Point."

"Ted," I screamed from between clenched teeth. "Turn around right now!" The three children joined the chorus. "Please, Daddy, turn around!" "Let's go back. Please, please, please!" "Pretty please with sugar on it?"

"You worry too much, honey! We'll make it. No problem! Now you kids be quiet and look at all the pretty scenery."

3.   Ted advances through the retreating traffic towards and into the tunnel. (reversal of initial barrier leading to high point of action)

Rounding a curve in the road we saw an unbelievable sight. A moving van had apparently gone up the road ahead of us. Undoubtedly a kindred spirit of Ted's and without a wife and three kids to nag him, he had decided to see for himself if he could make it through the tunnel. One glance at the mouth of the tunnel convinced him that it was not for him. He backed a mile or so down that narrow windy mountain road until he came at last to a place where the terrain on one side of the road was relatively flat and there was a slight clearing in the trees. Backing his truck off the road and up the slanting hillside, dodging trees, and blocking all traffic in both directions, the trucker maneuvered his truck back and forth, back and forth, until at last he had accomplished his 190-degree turn and was headed down the road away from the tunnel. A wise man he!

And then there was Ted.

"Turn around right here," I pleaded. "That trucker did it. You can, too." But Ted has never been easily discouraged, and he is willing to give things a try before he gives up.

At last we reached the tunnel. There were signs to the right of the opening and to the left. "Absolutely No Trucks Or Trailers!" "Narrow Tunnel!" "Low Clearance!"

"I can make it," the lunatic at the wheel said, and he headed straight for the mouth of the tunnel.

4. **With the support of his daughter and onlookers, Ted optimistically continues through the tunnel. (second reversal)**

I bit my lip, clenched my fists, and prayed. Ten-year-old Kristin, who had delighted in playing tour guide for the 1,500 or so miles since we had left home, suddenly became quiet for the first time. Eight-year-old Peter hid under the back bed. Only five-year-old Karen was supportive of her father. "Don't worry," she said. "I'm watching the walls!"

When people at both ends of the tunnel realized that Ted was going to try to drive the motor home through it, they jumped out of their cars and lined up to watch. They laughed and cheered and took pictures of us as Ted ever so slowly inched his way into the tunnel. The height proved to be no problem. We closed our ceiling vents, and there must have been at least four inches to spare between the top of our motor home and the ceiling of the tunnel. The sides of the tunnel were a different matter entirely. The walls were not smooth or lined with tiles as some tunnels are but were roughly hewn from the rock. Here and there were outcroppings. Ted turned the rear-view mirrors in so that they protruded as little as possible from the sides of the coach. He moved forward a few inches and then cranked the steering wheel to the right to maneuver around a rock sticking out of the tunnel wall. Creeping past that, he then found he had to crank the wheel to the left to avoid scraping an outcropping on our right. Dodging rocks on left and right, inch by miserable inch we moved through that tunnel.

5. **Ted drives the motor home slowly into an ever-narrowing tunnel to the point that it would appear that he is wedged between the walls. (catastrophe)**

I kept thinking, "This is it! We are going to get wedged in here like a cork in a wine bottle, and we will all die of suffocation. And someone is going to have to take our motor home apart bit by bit to get us out! And the authorities are going to throw us all in jail--or into an insane asylum. And we will never see our home again. How, oh, how did I ever end up married to a nut like Ted? How will I raise the children by myself after I divorce him? Or better yet, after I kill him!"

6. **Ted presses on to emerge successfully from the other side of the tunnel. (conflict resolved)**

Eventually, Ted worked his way around the last outcropping, and we reached the end of the tunnel. The crowd went crazy. They yelled and cheered and took our pictures. "Great driving!" they said. "That guy over there wasn't so lucky, though. He tried the same thing a few minutes ago and broke every window in his camper!"

Ted parked the coach, and we got out. He looked back through the tunnel and saw the crowd still standing at the other end laughing and talking about us. "Wow, that tunnel really does look narrow!" he said in amazement.

Soon we were on speaking terms again. Kristin got her voice back, and Peter came out from under the back bed. Karen's faith in her daddy continued unshaken. We had quite an adventure; one we would not soon forget.

Pretty exciting? You bet! If you think that was something, though, wait till I tell you about the time we took our motor home up higher than Ted's brother had ever had his airplane. But that's another story.

— Betty Stumpf

Now that you have read the story with the main points of the plot designated, you might want to ask yourself whether the author could have improved certain sections. Could she have done more with the catastrophe? Does the resolution come too quickly and too easily? Is there a real catastrophe, or is the catastrophe only in the mind of the wife?

Exercise 3-10

Use the following six outline sets either to analyze stories which you have read or to plot out the various details of a story which you are writing.

Outline 1

PLOT SCHEME:

State the basic problem of the story: _____

_____

_____

Describe the initial barrier: _____

_____

_____

State what the hero does to overcome the initial barrier: _____

_____

_____

Describe the high point of action where it seems the hero will overcome the initial barrier: _____

_____

_____

Describe the reversal:_____

_____

_____

Describe the catastrophe: _____

_____

_____

State what the hero does to emerge from near disaster and to resolve the basic problem: _____

_____

_____

Outline 2

PLOT SCHEME:

State the basic problem of the story: _____

_____

_____

Describe the initial barrier: _____

_____

_____

State what the hero does to overcome the initial barrier: _____

_____

_____

Describe the high point of action where it seems the hero will overcome the initial barrier: _____

_____

_____

Describe the reversal: _____

_____

_____

Describe the catastrophe: _____

_____

_____

State what the hero does to emerge from near disaster and to resolve the basic problem: _____

_____

_____

_____

Outline 3

PLOT SCHEME:

State the basic problem of the story: _____

_____

_____

Describe the initial barrier: _____

_____

_____

State what the hero does to overcome the initial barrier: _____

_____

_____

Describe the high point of action where it seems the hero will overcome the initial barrier: _____

_____

_____

Describe the reversal:_____

_____

_____

Describe the catastrophe: _____

_____

_____

State what the hero does to emerge from near disaster and to resolve the basic problem: _____

_____

_____

_____

Outline 4

PLOT SCHEME:

State the basic problem of the story: _____

_____

_____

Describe the initial barrier: _____

_____

_____

State what the hero does to overcome the initial barrier: _____

_____

_____

Describe the high point of action where it seems the hero will overcome the initial barrier: _____

_____

_____

Describe the reversal:_____

_____

_____

Describe the catastrophe: _____

_____

_____

State what the hero does to emerge from near disaster and to resolve the basic problem:

_____

_____

_____

PLOT SCHEME:

State the basic problem of the story: _____

_____

_____

Describe the initial barrier: _____

_____

_____

State what the hero does to overcome the initial barrier: _____

_____

_____

Describe the high point of action where it seems the hero will overcome the initial barrier: _____

_____

_____

Describe the reversal: _____

_____

_____

Describe the catastrophe: _____

_____

_____

State what the hero does to emerge from near disaster and to resolve the basic problem: _____

_____

_____

STEP THREE: ENHANCING CONFLICT

As family historians we are normally uncomfortable with many of the concepts of creative writing because we feel strongly that stories dealing with our family history must be factual. But family historians should consider the techniques of creative writing not as ways of altering the truth or an embellishment of the basic facts of the story, but rather an attempt to heighten in bold relief some of the interest-generating factual aspects of the story. This is particularly true of conflict. James Herriot used such an approach in *All Creatures Great and Small*. Mr. Herriot has two stories running simultaneously in this book: his attempt to establish himself as an animal doctor (a conflict with nature and often with the unbelieving Yorkshiremen whose livestock he services) and his romance with Helen Alderson (a conflict with himself and often with society at large). The first story dominates the beginning of the book, and the second story begins to appear only gradually towards the end and dominates the end of the book. He could have simply told some of his experiences as a veterinarian, and he could have excluded his love and happiness in courting and winning Helen. But without altering the truth of the historical facts, he carefully casts each story in a series of conflicts.

One example of this is his routine tuberculin testing of dairy herds. He could have factually stated that one of his many assignments involved the testing of dairy cows and could have explained the process, listed the numerous farms he had visited, calculated the time spent and the money earned and left it at that. Literally, these are the facts. Instead he chooses to present the facts, unaltered, in a story built around conflict. He sets up the conflict almost immediately:

> If I was kept waiting for ten minutes at every clinical while they got the cows in from
> the field it meant simply that after six visits I was running an hour late.

And we are off. Mr. Kay has not bothered to round up his herd. First, they coax them. Then they implore. They chase cows up and down the hills and finally try a dog. Nothing will work, and the constant struggle between man and cow rivets our attention. How will he solve his problem? After reversal, high point of action, and catastrophe, the farmer suggests a solution: the lad who can imitate a fly.

Sam propped his bicycle against the wall and paced solemnly forward. He made a circle of his thumb and forefinger and placed it to his lips. His cheeks worked as though he was getting everything into place then he took a deep breath. And, from nowhere it seemed came a sudden swelling of angry sound, a vicious humming and buzzing which made me look round in alarm for the enraged insect zooming in for the kill.

The effect on the heifers was electric.

> — James Herriot, *All Creatures Great and Small*

Another example of this process is Jean Shepherd's, "A Christmas Story," a television movie based on sections of his book *In God We Trust; All Others Pay Cash.* Shepherd could easily have detailed the specific facts, the dialogue, the sequence of events, but instead he constructs a story in which the facts are present in conflict sequences, and the details take on a life of their own.

Developing the Plot

In the brief exposition below, we are dealing with a family: a set of parents (Johannes Waller/Eva Catharina Stupfel), three daughters and two husbands (Anne Maria/Bernard Rueck, Magdalena/Johann Michael Meyer, and Marguerithe), and two sons and one wife (Joseph Antoine Waller/Magdalena Dauer and Bernhard Waller). Consider the main characters that make the plot work: the one brother (Joseph Antoine Waller) and two sisters (Anne Maria and Magdalena Waller) and the fact that we have a built-in rivalry or conflict that we can enhance.

The period of suffering had begun in 1828 and was to end in 1855, but the three surviving daughters of Johannes Waller and Eva Catharina Stupfel had no way of knowing in 1853 that the crisis would last only two more years; and even if they had known, they would have probably done little else except to endure whatever God was to send their way. Johannes and Eva Catharina Waller had had five daughters, but only three survived to maturity: Anne Maria, who married Bernard Rueck; Magdalena, who married Johann Michael Meyer; and Marguerithe. They had had three sons: Johann, who died when he was sixteen; and Joseph Antoine and Bernhard, who left Alsace, probably in 1839, for New York. The surviving sisters had remained in Alsace to continue the family while the surviving brothers had emigrated.

When Johannes Waller, the father, had died in 1826 at the early age of fifty the sons were still at home, but when in 1849 Eva Catharina, the mother, died at the age of sixty-eight, the two surviving brothers had been living in the United States for a decade. And communication was difficult. Bernhard had kept in contact by sending greetings via some mutual friends when he lived in Cincinnati, Ohio, but when their mother died, it took four more years for Joseph Antoine to learn of her death. The sisters had tried three times to reach Joseph Antoine. One letter they had sent registered, and two letters they themselves had taken to the post; but none had reached him. Fourteen years is a long time, and in the 1850s America was a very long way from Alsace, France; but somehow, Joseph Antoine learned of his mother's death, and forgotten relationships and obligations once again became very important. On 29 July 1985, he wrote a scathing letter accusing his sisters and their husbands of duplicity. Why had they not tried to reach him? Were they keeping him deliberately in the dark about her death so that they could inherit alone the family property?

And so on 14 August 1853, the three sisters, with their husbands, sat down to write two family letters, composed in several parts, which have survived to this day. The stamp has three postmarks: Wissembourg, Paris, and Le Havre. And it is addressed to Mr. Joseph Antoine Waller of Manitowac City in North America. It is little wonder that other letters had not survived. It is amazing that even this one managed to arrive and to survive the years. The letter is a plea for understanding and trust. After fourteen years, they still thought and worried about him. They wanted him to offer one son to God, presumably as a priest. They pleaded that he understand that they had not deceived and cheated him, that either an Englishman or more likely someone named Englaender had brought civil action against them in court for an old debt contracted by their mother, and this had apparently tied up the inheritance They continued that their mother had never been anything but just and that they had also been just.

Family Letter 1

Dear Brother:

Your authority has not arrived yet. Send the letter to Bernhard that is included in the letter to Joseph Anton Waller. Dear brother, we all send our heartiest greetings to you, your wife and children, and to our brother-in-law Bernhard Ruck and Michael Meyer; heartiest greetings to everyone from Anna Maria, Magdalena, Margareda Waller.

Much beloved brother Joseph Waller:

We sisters and brothers-in-law want to let you know that we are all still vigorous and healthy as the good Lord wishes. We have seen that all of you are also still healthy, and that makes us very happy.

We received your letter on the 29th. of July and noticed from the letter that you live in the forest.

We cannot write you enough that we all think of you and worry about you. But you are satisfied, and to be satisfied is rich. Have your children educated, and do not forget God; offer a child to the Lord, as it is from God.

And beloved brother, you wrote us that Bernhard wrote you that you were deceived and cheated. It was the Englishman (although Engländer is a name found in the Lauterbourg area); he wanted to cheat you, and he brought an action against us in court. Mother promised to pay him one guilder a year. He wanted to get that from us, but we did not approve of the idea. Then he really brought all guns to bear; he doesn't know anything—he's an asshead; he wanted to risk tremendous costs—a life of sorrows, but he didn't get a cent.

Didn't you ever know our mother. She wasn't unjust, and we haven't been so either. We would stand without fear before God. We wrote you, Joseph, and Bernhard everything four years ago when mother died about how everything turned out by three letters; two of them we took ourselves to the post and one we sent registered, but you didn't get them as you wrote.

And we haven't received a single letter from Bernhard. He had someone give us his greetings three times from Cincinnati where Beichms are.

Beloved brother, here at home everything is a large famine; you thresh a half a "sester" from nine sheaves, and the potatoes are rotting. It has been nine years since we had a good year, but still we managed to have fruit, but this year everything has turned to mildew and has hardly grown.

Dear brother-in-law:

I will put your matter in order as soon as I get the authority.

Dear Brother Joseph Waller:

Got a letter on the 11th. and am answering now, not for me alone but from everybody, and we are glad to hear that you are well. The dear God has cared for you and will go on, and we can say we are well also. We can count on God doing for us good if we are his children and always stay in that place. I can write you and say that we are in the will of God.

Have great harvest every year but this year everything has turned brown, but things are not so bad as we have laid by enough for this year. Please let us know how it goes with you.

And then on 14 December 1853, they wrote in a second letter that they had received Joseph's "Vollmacht" on authority and that they had forwarded 803 francs, presumably Joseph Antoine's portion of the estate. The financial and legal matters were apparently settled, but conditions in Alsace continued to be serious and difficult:

Family Letter 2

Much beloved brother Joseph Anton Waller:

We all want you to know that we are all still vigorous and healthy as long as the good Lord wishes and that we received your authority with the letter. We saw in the letter that you were convinced that we are all a bunch of deceivers. You have done us a grave injustice to think so. It is half from our brother-in-law the Englishman. If we could only talk with you, then you would really be surprised to hear what he has tried to do with us.

Dear Brother-in-Law:

I have taken care of your property (wealth or fortune) as well as I can. It comes to a sum of 802 or 803 francs.— When you have received your money, write immediately as you can for the receipt which will be made official by the authorities. Write whether you received the letter which I sent to you after you sent your first letter in 1853. My greetings to you and your wife and children. From your brother Bernhard.

These several letters present literally the only facts that we have, although there is a good deal of general information available on these difficult years.

Exercise 3-11

From the letters above, or preferably using documents that you have gathered about a person or event, isolate from the fact the inherent conflicts. For each conflict you isolate, circle the exact category of conflict that you are emphasizing, write out the conflict in your own words, and list the details of the conflict implied in these two letters or the documents at your disposal:

CONFLICT:

Man Versus Man, Himself, Society, Or Nature

Details of the conflict: _____

_____

_____

_____

_____

_____

CONFLICT:

Man Versus Man, Himself, Society, Or Nature

Details of the conflict: _____

_____

_____

_____

_____

_____

CONFLICT:

Man Versus Man, Himself, Society, Or Nature

Details of the conflict: _____

_____

_____

_____

_____

CONFLICT:

Man Versus Man, Himself, Society, Or Nature

Details of the conflict: _____

_____

_____

_____

_____

CONFLICT:

Man Versus Man, Himself, Society, Or Nature

Details of the conflict:

_____

_____

_____

_____

Sketch the Plot and Its Basic Conflict

One writer who worked by sketching out the plot before he wrote his final version—from general outline of the entire narrative through each chapter outline—was Gustave Flaubert, the author of *Madame Bovary*. For a more complete discussion of the plot as well as a fascinating discussion of the development of the novel from its initial rough outline through to its final version, refer to the Norton Critical Edition of *Madame Bovary*. In much the same way, we can begin with a journal written by William Grant and show how the journal or sections of the journal can be developed into a final narrative. First I jot down the flow of ideas from the entire journal, following exactly the sequence of events without augmenting or deemphasizing any one of the specific details. I have, however, broken the events of the journal into two parts and grouped the details of the first part into a story beginning with Grant's sitting for a portrait in 1885 and looking back over his life up to that point.

PART I: THE LAND OF OZ, UTAH 1838 TO 1885

> The story begins in American Fork. William Grant, 47, local merchant and civic leader sitting one wintery day in 1885 for his portrait. A small man, he always had large dreams and sees God and all the forces of nature conspiring together to fulfill his each and every dream. As the painter works, his mind wanders back over the successes of his life: birth on Christmas Day to the singing of carols; early childhood and his rejection of his parents' "vice" and intemperance. Development of an interest in Methodist Church and religious music at age seven (1–11). Cholera claims many members of his family while he survives through his strong religious faith (11–14). At age 13 he joins and advances through the ranks of the Mormon church (14–19). In his eighteenth year he becomes the director of a choir; proceeds to learn many new instruments/advances his musical education and has musical opportunities/considers himself a genius in music. Performs at Warwick Castle (16-26). He attaches himself to a girl named Eliza who shortly leaves him for another man/his first real loss—he leaves the Mormon church. Marries at 21 Harriet Foster; sets up home (19–25). Joins Willenhall Literary Institute and Willenhall Choral Society and Septette Band (24–26) and returns to the Mormon church. Journeys by ship and land to Utah (25–32); moves back to American Fork and opens music store/experiences prosperity (33–39); suffers a momentary setback when he loses postal appointment and is publicly shamed/suffers physically and psychologically (39–41); still he experiences business growth, performs civic duties, writes poetry, and undertakes and coordinates many musical events (41-55); but dark clouds are gathering with the start of polygamy persecution (67–69). The portrait is finished, and he leaves the studio.

PART II: THE LONE AND DREARY WORLD (1885–1916)

> The story continues with the now heightened persecutions of the U.S. government and his first arrest and subsequent trial in Provo for polygamy and three months in jail/ his indignant self-righteousness and defiant and strident religiosity/ his jail term one round of visiting, writing, preaching, music, and haughty defiance (July 1885-July 1886); returns home to an active life of business, musical, civic, and church duties (July 1886-July 1888); tragedy of death of his son (August 1888); now second arrest and seventeen-month jail term (April 1889 to August 1890); the manifesto and his sense of betrayal by the church (October 1890); the temple at Manti; dedication of SLC Temple (April 1892); sealed to his two wives (April 1893); financial struggle of the Emporium and constant deaths and funerals (Nov. 1890-). Treated poorly by the public. He collapses. Apostle Teasdale praises him. Runs successfully against a candidate supported by bishop; ward authority is against him. Death of Harriet Foster Grant, his wife.. Deseret News sues him. No longer asked to sing; lives among a strange people and has much to contend with; released as organist; anger\his mind crazed with the burden of debt. Finishes building his house. He is just worn out. Dropped from school board. Tired and weak, he finishes his building. Awarded a badge for 40 years of service (January

1900). Urged to resign his post as officer with schools because he cannot get to school on time; feels ignored. Failing health: loss of teeth, hard work and cold. Released as vice-president from American Fork Ward Choir. "I am getting old and tired." No longer called to speak and perform at funerals; seldom noticed for anything in a public way; business does pick up. Sam takes over running the store; has many new ideas for making money. Business now really picks up; William goes to England. Very successful trade in December. Does baptisms for the dead. Member of band commits suicide in 84th year. Old age has enfeebled him; is a nonentity; received much abuse and ill will. Only two more entries in his journal in January 1911 and July 1911. Dies in 1916.

Second, I isolate a general theme, beginning first with a series of related themes from Polti's list (*WFN* 42-48): plot theme 1—dealing with a threat; plot theme 3—overcoming or not overcoming an obstacle; plot theme 7—confronting a catastrophic circumstance; plot theme 11—being confronted with an obstacle to one's personal ambition. All of these seem to occur in the journal. To put it in terms of the four major conflicts normally found in a plot—man against himself, man, society, or nature—I see William Grant pitted against himself, his fellow man, the society in which he lives, and nature. Specifically, I choose to see the following theme in William Grant's journal: man is born into "A Land of Oz," a world filled with dreams that consume and fire his energies. He is anointed by the gods, addresses his flawed identity, sallies forth to fight evil, secures and marries the virgin maiden, sires children in his image, builds buildings and business, and contributes to empires, all in the illusive hope that he will somehow become identified with the immortal and the divine. But fortunes change and Grant's life becomes a treacherous journey into The Lone and Dreary World. He is incapable of turning back until he has drained his life force and been reduced to a forgotten grave. The tragedy of his life is that his dreams both grant him the power to embark on and complete his journey and render his efforts futile and self-destructive by obscuring his vision from the very happiness that is capable of bringing true and lasting joy.

Exercise 3-12

Now it is your turn. Returning to the journal or information you have gathered about a certain individual or event and using the pattern followed above, sketch out the overall plot with the details of the conflict included. At the end try isolating the general theme of the narrative that you have outlined.

The General Plot

_____

_____

_____

_____

_____

_____

_____

_____

_____

_____

_____

_____

_____

_____

_____

_____

_____

_____

_____

_____

The General Theme

_____

_____

_____

_____

_____

Developing the Outline

Many family historians have a deep suspicion of any creative rendering of an historical account; they consider any attempt to rewrite history as historical falsification. They want only the facts and the original documents transmitted in their historical purity. There is little doubt that some family historians have been particularly guilty of "cleaning up" historical documents. Fortunately only a limited few have gone so far as to misplace conveniently or lose damning pieces of information; however, many have concocted as well as written fanciful and largely erroneous accounts that, over a period of time, have confused researchers and made accurate family history difficult if not impossible. We are all familiar with the scores of legends and traditions that all families pass along from generation to generation. All of this, however, does not prevent a creative writer from developing a creative history as long as she is honest and clear about what she is doing and as long as she preserves the "truth" of the historical account. The goal is to tell the story well with narrative tension and illustrative dialogue and details, to bring the historical documents alive, and to experience the actual events. Consider first the journal entries below. While complete in one sense, they only hint at the emotion of the actual experience, even though they faithfully record all the particulars of the experience. Then consider the same details in a narrative form which allows us to experience the imprisonment with William.

The best way to illustrate this process is to work from an actual journal in writing a story. We have already outlined the total contents of the Grant journal. Reproducing and reworking the entire journal is beyond the scope of this workbook; dealing with a portion of the journal—Grant's time in prison—serves our purposes. There are actually two journals covering Grant's time in prison: the first was a daily record he kept while in prison, and the second was a more analytical account which he wrote when he returned home and was able to reflect on the prison experience. Because of the length of both sections dealing with Grant's time in prison, I have excerpted only portions of those sections, although I later will refer to several events which I have not excerpted.

Document I: William Grant's Daily Record of Life in the Pen

Second Term 3d indictment
20 months
April 20, 1889—

Sentenced at Provo, Utah Co
by Judge J.W. Judd—
for living with two wives

I was indicted for adultry and my Second wife for fornication. Both of us were Tried the same day, both convicted, I was sent to prison, she was dismissed, because her husband was in the pen.

1ST DAY APRIL 20, 1890—SATERDAY
At two P.M. I was Calld before Judge Judd, and after a short statement made to him stating the number and Condition of my family and that I had given evidence in my own case, and given the officers no trouble, I was soon sentancd to 20 months, left Provo on the D & R.G. Train at 4:15 with 7 other of our Bretheren in Charge of Deputy Redfield. reached salt Lake at 6 P.M. and was loaded with the rest into a heavy Wagon Bay & Baggage, arrived at Penitentiary at 7:20, went through the usual Examination and then

sent through the gates to the Charge of Mr. Doyle, he set me in a cell for the night of 2d with a Mr. H.H. Hawthorne, a gentile Polygamist. Mr Doyle Promised a Change for the next day if all the 8 Prisoners Came in to night. my Sentance was the longest Very much so.

2D DAY APRIL 21ST SUNDAY

I had a poor night and was glad to be let out this morning, ... among the first was Brothers Webb and Durrant, Mottt, and Cap Hart, was also recognized by 6 or 8 roughs who had been here, all the time since I left here in 1886, So hand shaking, and fraternity prevaild for an hour, Breakfast at 7:30 with Bro Webb who had Eggs for Breakfast. (being Easter Sunday) Visited and talked with Bro Durrant & Webb most of the day, telling them of home as they had been away Some 6 months, attended Sunday school at 9 a.m. and was invited to Join the Choir, and stayed to a rehearsall after School. Dinner at Noon, Beans & Bacon, at 3 P.M. In the evening we had the string Band out and I played with them in the yard. during the day Mr Doyle asignd me to my permanant Cell, No 112, 3d tier south, with a Brother Named John Thorpe of Logan. I could see out from my Cell many miles even to Am Fork, over the wall and all the farms, Houses, and Railroads and Smelters. Intervening, spent a pleasant evening—

3D DAY. MONDAY, APRIL 22D

Had a good nights rest, dreampt 3 times I was let free from here, got much more of an acquaintance with Brethren and made some new friends, orderd milk daily, had a long talk with Mr Doyle (gard) attended Band practice the Boys seem all delighted to have me here, especialy the musicians, several want me to teach a class. have gotin all my clothes &C from the Warden, and feel much more at home.

7TH DAY, FRIDAY, APRIL 26TH

Nice day, 3 hours of nuralga tied me to my cell. Bro Bailey, Bro Fox Lehi and some others left us for home, Choir Practice 2 P.M. and Band practice at 6 P.M. to day I read the Brief in Bro Nielsons Case before the supreme Court and thought it a Masterly argument.

24TH DAY, MONDAY MAY 13TH

This day the supreme Court is to give us a judgment in the Nielson Case Concerning our adultry status, and I am quite nervous all day, and Very unsettled—Very much talk, at 6 P.M. Comes a dispatch to Bro Nielson from S.F. Richards, "Your Case is won: and will have you freed Soon, that is all, and this causes a great sensation here, and we are all on the gruvive, talking and rejoicing all arround, as many expect to be effected therby, directly or Indirectly—we all are anxious to hear more to see if it hits our Case, and to learn if we are married or unmarried to our Wives, for whom we are here in prison.

25TH DAY, TUESDAY MAY 14

A fine morning, plenty of talking and hopeing, guessing and Chaffing all day all over the yard, for we Expect to go free. Choir practice at 2 P.M. at 7 P.M. Bro Hans Nielson the Contestant was set at Liberty Just as our gates was locking. we shouted good bye and good Luck—

26TH DAY, WENSDAY MAY 15

Wet stormy day. Still ancious for the Court News from Washington, but none comes, In cell reading nearly all the day.

49TH DAY, FRIDAY JUNE 7TH

A Very newsy day, and my faith and hopes went up 50 degrees by the news of arguments in the supreme Cout in the Barton Case, and three good Editorials in the Tribune in our favour, as well as Dr Ormsbys discharge that he could not be convicted of adultry for he had sufferd for Cohabitation. and I thought that sends me home, Soon after this attny Richards Came and Visited some Bretheren and he said it dont effect us a particle, So that sent me down below zero-locked up most of the day for Visitors.

303D DAY, SUNDAY, FEB 16

A queer day. No Sunday School- no Church. no dinner. the officers all Spent the day in making a thorough Search of house home and person. Our cells were ransacked, and al Boxes, Shelves, lives, and evry thing but the Bare walls taken. no Bible for every Book and paper was Caried out. One at a time our Clothes orderd from our Backs and searched. It took us an hour to make our Cell habitable and we had no dinner at all or any food from Breakfast till after 5 P.M. no Supper at all. Locked up all day—a prison Indeed. yea a Very hell.

423D DAY, MONDAY, JUNE 16TH

Working still on the well. at 6 P.M. a Terrible rush was made to drive all of us in our Cells and we were locked up when I found there had been a hole cut in the prison wall and Some got away, which caused a great Excitement. only one got of and he was Soon Brought Back and locked in the dungeon and rattled.

424TH DAY, TUESDAY JUNE 17

The hole in the foundation was repaired and new rules made none alowed to sit against or go to the Walls. Bp Stewart left for home. Choir met at night under my direction.

445TH DAY, TUESDAY, JULY 8TH

Another general flit here, and I am moved into Cell No 117 3d tier South, and I have it to myself. a good thing for me. Some new and stricter rules are adopted.

461ST DAY, THURSDAY, JULY 24TH

Pioneer day. the day I left prison here 4 years ago. I am feeling low and in a Very Meditative mood. all day no celebration here. out to work most of the day. all well.

487TH DAY, TUESDAY, AUGUST 19TH

My last day here as my sentance expires at midnight to night and I leave at 6 A.M. Tomorrow. Welcome this day. By the Kindness of the Barber and Bathman I get an Xtra Bath and shave. I got a nice hat rack to take home from Mr Williams the Barber. the Boyes are speaking words of good cheer all arround as I have been kind to and quite respectful to all. I am glad to leave them. I leave 20 of my Brethren here which I am sorry for. reviewing the past 16 months since I left home, I am thinking I have done exceedingly well, as this Brief record will show. I recieved 277 letters from my family and friends, during my stay here, part of which I retain to take home. my Visits number 164 from 86 differant persons. my presents I have not counted but they are quite numerous. all this leaves me under some obligations to my Kind friends and alone all to my father in heaven who has indeed been Kind and merciful to me, and to whom in closing this Brief and hasty record, I offer all praise.

Document II: Excerpts from the William Grant Journal

NOVEMBER 1888

Sunday, November 3, as I was very quietly returning from my Sabbath afternnoon sacrament services, upon reaching the corner of the church square, I was met by Deputy A.S. Marshall, W. Bennett, who very quietly informed me he had a warrant for my arrest for the crime of living with my wives and family. He said he did not have the warrant on his person but that it was in his office at Provo. He did not expect to arrest me or he would have brought it. He came over with others to arrest Bishop Bromley, but not being able to get him, he did not like to return empty handed so he took me. I told him alright that I was at his service. I asked the favor, however, that is often granted to others, to be let alone this night, it being the Sabbath, I was needed at church but I must go along, he said. I told him I would come over to the court the next morning but he refused unless I would bring over next day, sufficient witnesses to convict myself. This was beyond all reason, so I had to go to Provo on the Sunday night train. Dr. Hart, who was arrested 10 minutes after, at my door, also went along. We were placed in charge of the sheriff of the county, for the evening and were left at his house. Brother Thomas Fenters was very, very, kind to us. We had comfortable board and lodging. He even treated us to beer. I sang and played for them in the parlor for over an hour. The next day, Monday the 4th, we were taken before the U.S. Commissioner Hill on the usual charges. I waived examination and was ordered to get $1200 bonds which I had no trouble at all to get. Mr. Henry Davis, an old country friend, and Brother W.D. Roberts, my old bondsman, signing the bond. They searched all over for Rose but did not find her. They got her Brother Joseph and his wife and one other witness from Lake Shore against the Grand Jury. This was another great trial to our family but we still felt resonably well about it. Rose was at Mona at Brother Jone's and I wrote her to come home at once which she did and once more we are all together on our own lot and will have peace for a short time at all events.

This was a busy month, as the holidays are approaching fast.

DECEMBER 1889

Christmas month and in the Prison. the thought is horrible, for it is my harvest month, my Birth month, my Wedding month and the thoughts worry me to sickness, headache &c. yet the month past quick and pleasantly under all the circumstances. I was Buisy at my Books and Pen. the 23d was a notable day, a general Fast day for all the church and the Brethren in prison all Fasted. I read 887 Verses of my Bible got a headache but fasted and prayed Earnestly for Gods mercy and Blessings—Soon Xmas day Came and we had another grand treat from friends in the City of Salt Lake, plenty food rich and good, also a Concert by the salt Lake glee Club &c—I got many letters and other Kind remembrances from family and friends. I Composed several Poems this month one to Each of my Wives and a Comic one Dr Isaacsons Baby's nose. the year Past in a Solemn manner to me for my reflections made me serious—my last act was a letter to my Friend Dr. E. Isaacson—

AUGUST 1890

Month of Liberty to me. Rules still stricter, and I am not to go outside at all now, but spend my time well with music and Literature. the best of it is all our Elders are going home and I hope may not Come here anymore. We are not allowed the use of our Iron Cells now, but locked out homeless, except at night a great hardship and no sense in it at all to me. I am exasperated—but as my time is getting Very short, I propose to Bear with all patiently. I am Counting days and meals and almost hours as I march in the Dry yard in the Scorching Sun, My Brethren are Very Kind to me. 19 of them go home this month, God be Praised. at length the 19 day Came and my record says, 487th day. August 19, My last day here. Welcome, Welcome. Bathed and Shaved. got a nice Hat rack worth $5.00 from the Barber, and Bro Hans Jasperson presented me with a nice Watch Chain made by his hand from his familys hair. all the Boys are speaking words of good Cheer to me. I done Exceedingly well while here, all think and say. I got 277 letters sent me, 164 Visits from 86 differant persons. all this leaves me under some obligations to them. my Presents are quite numerous and I am happy at having so many tokens from my thousands of friends. I am grateful and above all thankful to my heavenly father for his merciful Kindness to me to whom in Closing this Brief record I offer all Praise—W. Grant.

I was set free next day and was treated Very Kindly by many. Bro W.B. Smith met me at the Prison and helped me off. Bp Scow saw me from the grounds. I got free ride to the city, free Breakfast and dinner at Bro S.F. Balls. all were rejoiced to see me a free man. done some Buisness and got home on the U.P. Train at 5:40 where I met my loved ones and was greeted Kindly by all. I now Begin my usual Labors in the store and home dutys, and find plenty to do—I will mention here I attend servise on Sunday at our Church, but the Bp did not invite me to Speak and I felt very much hurt. niether did he ask my report at any time—

SEPTEMBER 1890

Work, Work, Work. No End of it. Visited a few friends to Welcome me home. Many had died while I was away, others still dying. I attended funerals, Sabbath Schools, music and other meetings, and it took a month to get through greeting my friends. I preached a Short adress by request at Bro Bushs funeral—administerd to the sick all over and was Buisy all the month.

OCTOBER 1890

Went to October Conferance. Saw many friends and it was an interesting time as the great Manifesto on Polygamy was Brought before the church. I heard it all, but was mystified and Cannot say I was pleased at all, though I held up my hand to aggree that Pres Woodruff should have the right to Issue it and that I would not oppose it but I hated it. Still Buisy with work and meetings. attended several funerals and much other Public work for the interest of the salvation and happifying of the Souls of men, for I take great delight in these labors—

The next step is to rough-out a detailed outline using these sections of the journal. Each story, even as a section of the complete journal, can contain several scenes; remember to think of a scene as the introduction of a new character, the "French scene" (*WFN* 106). The development of a narrative is an organic, living experience. Themes shift, characters grow, and plots alter before your very eyes. So, even though I have a general theme for the complete journal, I first construct a theme for the section I am writing, William Grant's second prison sentence.

> Chapter Theme: William Grant, a polygamist, is arrested and imprisoned by the U.S. Government for practicing plural marriage; he must overcome or be overcome himself by imprisonment and the ramifications of imprisonment—initially its physical confinement but more importantly and increasingly with time, the public shame and emotional trauma that imprisonment brings.

I sketch the story as a *W*:

First, the intent: William Grant, a practicing polygamist, is confronted with arrest and the possibility of imprisonment, the barrier or obstacle which he seeks to avoid.

Second, the barrier: Grant is arrested and though he seeks to avoid imprisonment, he is sent to prison.

The barrier is reversed: Grant is sent to prison, but he actively believes in his imminent release and in his innocence as charged: that he is neither an adulterer nor a bigamist but a respectably married man who is practicing polygamy according to his conscience.

There is a high point of action and hope sets in: Grant expects the Supreme Court to reverse the Edmund Tucker Act and that he will momentarily be released and allowed to reenter society as an innocent and respectable man.

Second reversal or reversals: a series of prison reversals, and Grant reluctantly accepts that he will serve the full term; still he holds to his belief that he is not a criminal, but an innocent man.

Then the catastrophe: Grant is released, but the Church's abandonment of polygamy leaves Grant deprived of his moral validation and clearly labeled a bigamist, a common criminal.

Finally the resolution: Grant returns home defeated, having realized the full implications of a prison sentence, its physical confinement as well as its emotional trauma.

A story devoted to an almost two-year prison term would be too long; so I begin with the conference at which the famous manifesto was announced and return Grant through a flashback to the events of his prison sentence. Now I can sketch out the sequence of events. (Note that, to conserve space, several items noted in the outline were not mentioned in the journal excerpts.)

it is conference, October of 1890

Grant travels by train from American Fork to Salt Lake City

his mind wanders back over the events of the past twenty months

his wife's arrest

his arrest at the depot

his trial in Provo

how Apostle Lyman took his hand as he boarded the D & RG Railway in American Fork to travel to Provo for his sentencing.

his journey by train to Salt Lake City

the pen wagon waiting at the depot to take him to the Mud Palace

his pedigree taken and then he is sent inside

first he is placed on the 3rd tier, north

then he is transferred to Cell 112, 3rd tier south, opposite and facing home

he could lie in his hammock and gaze across to Utah Valley

his arrest and imprisonment

the series of reversals he experiences while in prison:

> no supreme court decision (days 24-25)

> fellow convict commits suicide (days 36-37)

> there is no release; he is "set down" (day 49)

settles into a monotonous sixteen-month routine of weather reports, headaches, shaving, baths, haircuts, watching others go home, writing music and letters, receiving letters and visitors, reading, meeting with his choir and band, working on the pump by day as well as by night, and listing the foods he receives from friends: fish, beef, green peas, peaches, currants, gooseberries, bananas, lemons, cheese, butter, apples, milk, and strawberries.

he realizes the uncertainty of life (day 255)

his cell is turned upside down by the guards (day 303)

there is a prison break (days 423-424)

ever stricter rules (day 445)

feeling low (day 461)

his summary: 277 letters and 164 visits from 86 persons (day 487)

now as he walks up towards the Tabernacle from the depot, he sights and greets old friends; when he reaches the Tabernacle, he finds himself enveloped in friends, but he is still troubled because only last month, after being released from prison, the bishop had not called on him to speak in church he senses a strange distance between him and his former friends; it is almost as if they are avoiding him

conference commences; prayer and then music; and then the Manifesto

he raises his hand to support it; but he hates it in his heart

In the first version of the outline, I have only hinted at some things which I will probably elaborate in the final prose version, and expressed more detail about items that I might well play down or ignore in the final version. The point is, however, that I have made a start.

Exercise 3-13

Taking the general plot you recorded in exercise 3-12, sketch out the sequence of events or write a more detailed outline of the section or limited story you are developing. It is important that you limit your narrative to a certain event or section of a person's life. Later, when you have become adept at writing about a portion or section of a person's life or about a specific event, you will want to attempt the more ambitious and complicated task of writing a person's biography or of linking several events into an historical narrative.

_____

_____

_____

_____

_____

_____

_____

_____

_____

_____

_____

FROM OUTLINE TO PROSE

Your task is now to turn your outline into a prose narrative, but before you write your story, consider the following prose version. I have written this section of the William Grant journal as a story in third person, limited, and as the outline indicates, I have restricted the action to one day, actually a morning ride from American Fork to Salt Lake City and a morning Mormon general conference meeting in the Salt Lake Tabernacle. This limitation gives the story more unity; a chapter devoted to eighteen months would simply stretch the action out too far. I have included the eighteen-month jail sentence through the device of flashbacks: William reminisces as he journeys toward Salt Lake City and considers the Manifesto abolishing polygamy that will fall into his life as a thunderbolt out of the blue.

The Betrayal of William Grant

William Grant waited in the early morning light for the train to Salt Lake City. The sun, hanging somewhere in the East, would soon mount the peaks of the Wasatch Range and pierce down through the canyons and out onto the valley floor. With its warmth, the darkness of the night would reluctantly retreat first from the fragile communities of the Saints now filling up the land between the mountains and the placid but violently unpredictable lake, then from the surface of the Lake's dark waters, and finally out into the empty waste of the western desert; life could begin anew.

William pulled his watch from his pocket and listened to the sounds of the retreating darkness: the animals on the farms that lay just outside the town of American Fork and the movements of people as they made fires, boiled pots, and placed food on tables. Kneeling down, he touched his hand to the track and felt the shock of its coldness and the comforting vibrations of the approaching train. By 1890, the grandiose Mormon State of Deseret that had extended north to include parts of Oregon, Idaho, and Wyoming, westward to include all of Nevada and part of California, southward to include most of Arizona and part of New Mexico, and eastward to include part of Colorado had become a diminished vision, the Territory of Utah. In 1884, the U.S. government had moved aggressively to punish those who practiced polygamy, and then in February 1887, the infamous Edwards-Tucker Act had given federal authorities the power they needed to bring the Mormon church to heel. Mormon railroads had been part of that original vision. The Mormons had built them without government aid and with their own bare hands only to have eastern financiers through the Union Pacific buy up and eliminate the uncooperative and competitive railroads, and they, like all else in Utah, were now slipping from Mormon control. Still, to William Grant, it was their railroad— if not in fact at least in name. A locomotive with the brave statement "Utah Central Railway" pulled slowly now alongside the depot siding, its diamond-shaped smokestack belching its combination of steam and smoke into the frigid air, and came to a lurching stop.

William Grant had been free for only one month, a free man after seventeen months in prison—487 days in the "Mud Palace" at Sugarhouse. Time enough to receive 277 letters, 164 visits from 86 persons, and presents from friends too countless even to remember. And now free to move where he wished and how he wished, free to board a train for Salt Lake City, to link arms with those who with him had fought the oppressors, the persecutors who had driven him and others from their homes and harassed and vexed those who had lived God's celestial law.

He stepped up onto the iron platform and into the car, stopping briefly to warm himself at the large pot-bellied stove. The last time he had taken the train to Salt Lake City he had been in chains, and he had sat where he had been told to sit; now he moved without restraint about the warm railway car—to sit where he wanted and with whom he wanted.

When he had been released, Brother Balls had met him at the prison, seen him from the grounds, and given him a ride from Sugarhouse to downtown Salt Lake; he had even given him a free breakfast and dinner. When he arrived home in American Fork at 5:40 P.M. on the Union Pacific, he had noticed that some of his closest friends had not been there to greet him, but his family, the loved ones he had suffered for, had been there. The others had probably been caring for their own families, and he had felt complete knowing that his family had remained strong and faithful throughout his long vigil. When the Sabbath had rolled around, he had dressed carefully, pleased that he still cut a smart figure after seventeen months in prison and had marched over to the church with his family, greeting old acquaintances as a returning hero. As the service began, he had sat anxiously aware that all the eyes of the church were on him, anticipating with pride his report to the congregation. He had already prepared in his mind what he planned to say, almost forgetting the countless days of boredom as he mentally rehearsed his many trials and tokens of suffering and his friends and their visits and hundreds of letters. But the church meeting had droned on, and the bishop had not asked him to report.

After the service, he had stood in the door of the church building, and he thought that the handshakes were not as quick, the grips not as strong, the eyes not as direct as they had seemed when he had marched off to do battle with the marshalls and sheriffs of hell seventeen months before. Sabbaths of August gave way to the Sabbaths of September, and still the bishop had not asked for his report. And he had begun to notice that while old friends still came by the store, still gave him their business, still listened to his litany of sufferings, their eyes seemed to wander purposefully over the glassware in the counters, the canned and bottled goods on the shelves, and the paraphernalia hanging from the ceiling of the room, changing the subject of conversation with their very movements when he referred to his time in prison. Gradually he had come to realize that there really was no interest in his report, that in fact his detailed descriptions of boring prison routine, suicides and prison breaks, and surly guards rattling the cells of expressionless convicts seemed almost to embarrass those who dropped by his store. With that growing realization a confused pain would rise from his stomach, up into his throat, giving him another of his crippling migraine headaches.

The train now left the flat farmland and began the slow climb up to the Point of the Mountain. As it climbed, Utah Lake came more and more into view. It filled almost half of the valley and, like some primitive and unpredictable animal, it seemed to lick at the edges of life, the countless farms and homes that checkered the valley floor and braved the lake's unpredictable waters that after heavy snows would rise up to drown the farms that had dared to approach too closely. As the track reached the top of the grade, William looked out the dirty window through hazy early morning light back on the broad expanse of Utah Valley, across to the far side of the lake where on a lazy, late Sabbath afternoon two summers ago he had watched helplessly at a family picnic as his son Tommy, playing in the inviting waters, had accidentally stepped into a sink hole and had slipped before his very eyes into the water's darkness. They had searched until the sun had gone down into the night before giving up; even farmers in the area had brought torches and small boats, but they had not been able to find the boy's body. And the next morning as suddenly as the lake had swallowed up his son and sucked out his life during the night, it vomited up Tommy's lifeless form. As William had lifted the body and gently cradled the head of the boy, a slight trickle of blood ran down from his son's mouth and across William's sleeve.

Suddenly the sun struck the tops of the mountains, and its warming rays flowed out onto the now peaceful and placid lake. The train rounded the Point of the Mountain, and Utah Lake slipped from his view.

William's arrest had been a sudden and unforeseen accident too, crashing into his life on an equally placid and peaceful Sabbath afternoon. The storm had been stirring deep below the tranquil surface for months, and William had heard plenty of rumors that he might be arrested at any time; but it still came on him as unexpected and unannounced as the drowning of his son. He was on his way to church when Deputy Bennett accosted him.

"I didn't expect to see you, Mr. Grant. I come to arrest Bromley; but you'll have to do. I got a warrant for your arrest back in the office; I'll get Bromley later."

"Marshall Bennett," William protested, "it's the Sabbath. I'm needed at church. Let me spend the Sabbath with my family."

"Nothing doin'; I come to get you, and you must come along."

Despite William's promise that he would voluntarily give himself up on Monday, the deputy marshall had insisted on taking William with him. William quickly posted a bond of $1,200 and returned home to resume his life of civic service and private charity as well as to run up a decent Christmas profit at his business, Grant's Music Emporium and Novelty Bazaar. Friends and family gathered for two days at Christmas to celebrate his fiftieth birthday and do him honor. Following the christmas season, he gathered the elderly of his community at an old folks party, preached a grand sermon at a funeral of a friend, delivered a series of lectures on the life of Christ, attended a concert in Salt Lake City where he sang a new song each night, organized a concert for the Sunday school, wrote and published a new song, feted a grand ball for 120 friends in his own concert hall, and spoke at a funeral for a child which had been smothered by its mother. But all during the Christmas season and his frenetic activities of the new year, he had brooded on the death of Tommy, his arrest, and an almost certain prison sentence.

The train was now along the face of the Point of the Mountain, parallel to the Jordan River, the tributary that like a joke of nature emptied the living waters of Utah Lake into the crystalline death of the Great Salt Lake, living waters that could swallow up his son into the dead waters of a lake that would allow nothing to sink below its surface. He could still see his friends combing the lake, looking for the body, and later helping bury the boy. The night before his sentencing these same friends had held a reception for him in the Church meetinghouse. Someone had passed the hat and collected almost $30 to help him through the troubled times ahead.

Then on Saturday morning, as he stepped onto the cars of the train for the short trip to Provo to be sentenced, none other than Apostle Lyman had taken his hand and sat with him all the way to Provo. His success as a proprietor of the largest music emporium in the area and his faithfulness and devotion to the cause had reached the highest echelons of the church. Lyman had even ordered an organ. That day the whole matter had sat lightly on him, so lightly that he spent the hours before his sentencing leisurely attending a teachers' meeting at the central school and later enjoying a noon-day dinner with Brother Devys. He felt brave and strong as he marched up to the Provo courthouse at two o'clock to confront Judge Judd and his gentile law.

"What do you have to say?"

"Your honor, I have a large family and a large business interest. In all my dealings, I've given the officers no trouble, and in my trial I've given all the evidence myself. I hope you'll be lenient."

"Twenty months," banged the gavel.

Of all those sentences meted out that day, his had been the longest. The room was silent, and William's brave self-control began to falter a bit; but he was too shocked to grasp the full impact of the number twenty. He simply stared at the judge.

"And the costs of the court," he heard the clerk add into the bargain.

"Of course," and the judge turned his attention to the next case.

Someone took William from behind, and as he had turned he looked up into Deputy Redfield's face, a tall, almost emotionless officer of the court. Redfield scurried the little band of convicted felons along the walks and streets of Provo and into the depot where William, along with seven other men, found themselves chained together as they boarded the 4:15 P.M. Denver and Rio Grande Railway train for Salt Lake City. When the train made a momentary stop at American Fork, several of his children and friends were there to greet him. To their tears and deeply concerned faces, William had bid a cheerful adieu; he knew he had done no wrong, and he could not help but believe that he would shortly be free.

At about six o'clock the train came to a halt in the Denver and Rio Grande Terminal several blocks west of downtown Salt Lake, and William could see the pen wagon with its restless team through the window of the railway car. With each transfer, he was taken farther and farther away from his home and his friends and deeper and deeper into the hole that was to be his home for seventeen months.

It took almost an hour for the horses to drag the heavy wagon filled with men and baggage through the streets of Salt Lake from the main part of town and up to the Utah State Penitentiary at Sugarhouse. William could make out the fifteen-foot high walls of the infamous "Mud Palace," his home for the next 487 days. The penitentiary wagon halted in front of a small six-sided outbuilding. It was now early evening, and each man stumbled as he came off the wagon. The guards pushed them into a line of eight and proceeded to register each as they recorded each man's vital statistics. In the late shadows of the day, a guard moved back the heavy door of the main gate, and William passed into the even deeper darkness of the prison yard.

The prison house was built of brick, heated in winter by steam, but summer was now coming on, and there was little that could be done to ward off the devastating heat. A central corridor ran between the cell blocks, then a long iron-enclosed corridor, and finally a set of iron bars for each cell. There were two cell blocks of three tiers or rows of cells, twenty on each tier. One set of cells faced south, and one faced north. Each cell was equipped with two hammocks or bunks, and at one end of the prison house there was a connecting passageway to the dining hall. William spent the first night in the north cell block, third and uppermost tier, with a certain H.H. Hawthorne. He slept poorly as he adjusted to sleeping in a hammock. William was fifty years old, not particularly old, but old enough to find the prospect of a term in prison daunting. His migraine headaches were a constant plague, he was feeling now the increasing aches of age, and he worried constantly about his first wife's failing health. To make matters worse, most of his friends were on the upper two tiers, facing south; he was isolated from his fellow polygamists in a cell facing north.

The next morning William awoke cold, tired, and sore, but when he joined the other prisoners in the dining hall, his spirits began to pick up. It was Easter Sunday, and there was a glorious breakfast of eggs. At the noon meal, the guard Doyle stopped Grant and said that he would keep his promise and change him to the block facing south. William carefully packed his few belongings after Easter Sunday service and waited almost an hour in his old cell for Doyle to appear. The heavy bar doors to the outer corridor and then to his cell opened, and Doyle called to Grant to come out. Taking his belongings in his arms, William and Doyle together walked along the iron walkway, down the staircase, across the asphalt floor to the south cell block and up to the third tier, Cell 112; his new cell mate was a fellow polygamist named Thorpe from Logan. All the rest of that afternoon and into the evening, William lay in his hammock gazing out towards the Point of the Mountain and American Fork, over the walls, past all the farms, houses, railroads, and factories. Locked in a pleasant revelry, he spent the evening imagining his store, Grant's Emporium, with its vast assortment of musical instruments; piles of packaged merchandise; the mobiles, festive crepe paper, and miniature dolls dangling in grand confusion from the ceiling; and the oil lamps, fine crockery, and dishware. He even imagined that he could see the lights of his home, his wives' delicious cooking, the faces of his children, and the sweetness of the spring evening. That night he fell easily to sleep and spent a restful night, dreaming three times that he had been set free.

When he awoke the morning of his third day in prison, a strange sense of hope had seized him. His last term had lasted only a few weeks, and there was constant talk about the Nielson and Barton cases now before the Supreme Court arguing that polygamy was not adultery. And it was not long before someone got hold of a newspaper with the entire brief reprinted. The brief was a masterly argument destroying all the arguments of the gentiles. If the Supreme Court would see the logic of the brief and rule that polygamy was not adultery, then William and the others could be free and home in a few weeks.

Gathering courage and strength, he threw himself into a constant round of music classes, concerts, and social gatherings. With each new meeting of the prison band and the choir, his spirits soared. It was hardly freedom, but as the days wore into weeks, the band and choir sustained William and earned him extra privileges. Many an evening he was away from his cell in the dining room until nine o'clock practicing music until his very heart sang. But the constant rumors that the Supreme Court was now hearing arguments against the equating of polygamy with adultery lifted his spirits from the heavy anchor of reality. Even the Mormon-hostile *Tribune* had three editorials in the polygamist's favor.

And then on his forty-ninth day in prison, Dr. Ormsby was discharged because of a court ruling that cohabitation had not, in his case, constituted adultery; William's spirits were irrepressible. Several prisoners began to congratulate themselves on their imminent discharge. Matters reached almost a fever pitch by the noon meal; and later rumors raced from cell to cell. But just when he had convinced himself that he would soon be discharged, an attorney named Richards asked to speak with several of the prisoners that he was representing: "Don't get your hopes up, boys; Ormsby's case has nothing to do with you."

Now the routine of prison life had begun to take hold of William's mind. A convict committed suicide, and William could hear his bellowing like a bull echoing between the northern and the southern blocks. News of old friends on the outside dying trickled into his world, and he recognized how his isolation prevented him from succoring those left behind with his popular and often requested funeral orations. The guards periodically ransacked the cells looking for what-only-Heaven-knew; it took William almost an hour each time to clean up the mess. Then the guards found a hole in one wall, and one prisoner got away in the ensuing confusion. The guards found him, threw him into the dungeon, and rattled his cage. And they then imposed even stricter rules which made life almost hell for William.

The gradual braking of the train brought William back to the present. Scores of people filled the Salt Lake Depot and the streets that led up to Temple Square, and William felt himself swept along as the crowd made its way to the Tabernacle. He greeted and embraced old friends, met and made new ones, and took his seat with the tried and the tested. The meeting began: the prayer, the music, and then some opening remarks; but everyone was waiting for the aged prophet, Wilford Woodruff, to rise. As the voice of God on earth, Wilford Woodruff would have words of sustenance and guidance to give the army of faithful. Then slowly, the old man rose from his seat. It was as if all eyes above, below, and on the earth were fixed on his every movement. No one would have judged him impressive as he made his way almost confusedly to the stand. Bent low with age and broken by over four years in exile and flight, Wilford Woodruff was even less impressive when he spoke. His high, thin voice echoed across the cavernous void of the Tabernacle as he chronicled the persecutions and the punishment that the Saints had endured because of their stubborn insistence on polygamy: "And I now publicly declare that my advice to the Latter-day Saints is to refrain from contracting any marriage forbidden by the law of the land." Before anyone had a moment to consider the import and the implication of his words, Lorenzo Snow moved to Woodruff's side:

"I move that, recognizing Wilford Woodruff as . . .," and William was vaguely conscious that he raised his right arm up in a sustaining motion, automatically . . .

obediently and without enthusiasm. Indeed, he felt a keen pain pierce his heart, and deep down he felt betrayed.

The rest of the meeting was a blur. The choir sang the closing hymn, someone prayed, and William felt himself moving or being moved towards one of the numerous exits. As he emerged into the glare of day, the sudden light confused his eyes, and for a brief moment he imagined that he was still dressed in his prison stripes. As he stumbled on the small step that emptied him and others out onto the Temple grounds, he thought he was stumbling out of his cell into the glaring light of the prison yard. He was grateful for his momentary confusion because he knew that everyone else could not see, and he wanted to be left alone as he struggled with the anger and the pain that had begun with the sustaining vote and had by now worked its way up into his brain as another penetrating headache. He passed the unfinished temple, still surrounded by workmen's tools and scaffolding, and found himself momentarily outside the Temple wall on the street, moving down the slight hill toward the train depot.

If he saw or passed anyone he knew, he was absolutely unaware. He was too confused, too stunned even to lift his eyes from the ground. And when he boarded the waiting train, he found a seat away from the other passengers where he could stare at the window. The locomotive's wheels spun, the force of the engine's pull passing itself back through the coupling of each car; and then the metallic reaction as each car resisted the pull of the engine; and finally the obedient line of cars began to move forward in one coordinated but resistant drag, out across the Salt Lake Valley toward the Point of the Mountain.

The small farms and isolated homes stood like forgotten and forsaken sentinels, and William felt alone as he could never remember feeling in his entire life. Utter and absolute defeat filled his soul as he tried to fit together the years of emotional suffering and physical sacrifice he had laid down in making "The Principle" of polygamy a living and human reality. Now he understood why the bishop had not asked him to speak to his congregation upon his release. William Grant was a living embarrassment and a painful reminder of a now strange and peculiar practice that everyone was scrambling to forget and leave behind. The train rounded the curve of the Point of the Mountain and moved along the bench—the high water mark of the ancient, prehistoric lake that had once filled the entire valley. William could see below the homes and farms of American Fork and beyond that Utah Lake now sinking rapidly into a gloomy darkness, a vision of treachery and deceit.

It was dark when the train ground and clanked to a halt at the American Fork station. The sun had dropped into the western desert, and the day was no more. The brief light of the depot confused his eyes, and when his son Will stepped forward to take his arm, William was momentarily startled. It took a few seconds for William to adjust his eyes to the darkness of the street, and his son gently guided him and alternately let him find his own way. In each of the windows of the homes along the street, William could make out an oil lamp or a single electric bulb, and he could detect people sitting or moving about in the light that came from each home. He knew that Will would have carefully locked the doors of the Emporium, accounted for the moneys and the inventory, cleaned up the confusion and mess of the day and prepared to meet the traffic of the next day. He also knew that both of his wives and most of his children would be home and that supper would be ready as usual. He walked now silently beside his son, and as he walked he saw the dark outline of Grant's Music Emporium and Novelty Bazaar and, above the Emporium, the lights of his apartments. Everything had changed and yet nothing had changed. He had left American Fork in the morning as God's martyr and true soldier and had returned home an adulterer and a bigamist, a common criminal.

Before you can try your hand at writing some scenes, you must decide how you plan to begin your story. Up to this point, we have considered the story as if it were one correctly ordered chronological sequence, opening with the first event in time and ending with the last event in time. Many writers begin their stories, however, at points other than the chronological beginning of events.

STEP FOUR: BEGINNING THE NARRATIVE

It is almost impossible to conceive of a successful story without a good beginning, especially in today's world of instant gratification. In fact, it is universally held that if the author does not know how to begin the story well, he probably does not know how to tell the story well. But before we can consider how to begin a story, we have to settle the issue of how to handle time: with correct chronological order, with a number of flashbacks, with a series of shifts in time, or with a frame.

There are several ways to describe the opening: opening with a dramatic question, getting started fast, presenting the baited hook, etc. Perhaps the term "baited hook" with all of its fishing references is the easiest to understand. These all describe the same basic concept: put your main character immediately in front of the reader, present or at least hint at the basic problem of the story, and drop the reader into the setting. In other words, we do not begin at the true beginning of the story. We consciously reach into the story itself to find some incident or scene that will bait the reader into taking the hook or reading the story. Each of the following examples is taken from a writer of family history.

The Baited Hook of Character

By half past noon, the old man had finished his dinner and started through the house to the front porch. His narrow shoulders were hunched over an aluminum walker which he thrust ahead of him after each deliberate step. All about, people stood or sat in little clusters, talking, laughing. Their voices were a blended babble to his ears, their faces an unfocused blur to his watery blue eyes. They made way for him as he approached, and then watched in respectful silence as he shuffled through the living room and out the screen door.

He slumped down heavily in his accustomed chair, a painted wooden rocker, from which he could lean forward and spit tobacco juice into the grass. With a small pocket knife, he carved a dark chunk of Day's Work, his favorite plug, and stuck it between his toothless gums. The spring air was warm and humid, and no breeze stirred in the porch shade, but the old man seemed not to mind; neither the weather nor his labored walk through the house had brought sweat to his brow.

There was in his appearance a curiously contrasting show of forcefulness and vulnerability, a mingling of durable and fragile features. He was neatly dressed in a dark blue linen suit, a gold shirt that fit loosely about his thin neck, a multicolored nylon tie with a fist-sized knot, and a polished pair of wing-tip cordovan shoes. He clutched a tobacco-stained handkerchief in his gnarled hands. His hair—what remained of it—grew in a narrow fringe above his collar; it was as soft and fine as duck down, and its color matched the stark whiteness of his eyebrows. Warm sunshine had given his face and scalp a healthy-looking touch of tan, and veins in his temples stood out beneath his translucent skin with the blue-under-brown softness of a candled egg. His habitual smile often broke into laughter, and when he spoke, his voice was resonant with strength and good cheer.

"Well, I'm 102 years and two days old today, but I feel fifty years younger," he sang out, looking around into the hazy sea of faces. "You reckon I'll live another century?"

— John Egerton, "An American Family"

Another example.

Bess of Hardwick was the most remarkable woman in Elizabethan England, of chief historic interest, after the two Queens, Elizabeth I and Mary Queen of Scots, with both of whom she was intimately acquainted over the years. She was the grandest woman builder England has ever known, having built the new Hardwick Hall—loveliest of Elizabethan houses—as well as largely rebuilt the old Hall there; she also built the contemporary Chatsworth, a splendid house which later dukes of Devonshire replaced with their present palace. Only her friend Lord Burghley surpassed her in the scale of his building—as he said of himself, "never out of bricks and mortar." The same might be said of her.

— A.L. Rowse, *Eminent Elizabethans*

Exercise 3-14

Try your hand at composing an introduction that centers on a certain character.

_____

_____

_____

_____

_____

_____

_____

_____

_____

_____

_____

The Baited Hook of Unusual Ideas

I lived before I was born. And this living was a great deal more than some vaporous gene waiting to settle itself into some darkly mortal embryo. I was full statured, totally conscious, and in control of every thinking faculty. Before the earth was formed, I lived. When it was shadowy gas in the cosmos, I lived. In that ancient and solemn time, I walked, I talked, and I made my conscious choice—and lucky for me, my choice was the right one.

Apparently I was endowed, in this pre-mortal existence, with considerably more wisdom than I was later to know in mortality. I made no mistakes in my pre-existent state. It was after I was born that the record of my errors grew.

— Paul Bailey, "Polygamy was Better than Monotony"

Once again, we have the main character, we know the problem, his "record of . . . errors," and we know the setting, Mormon culture.

Another example. In the midst of a mid-nineteenth-century visit to England, the poet James Russell Lowell attempted to trace the deeply buried roots of his family tree. His findings were recorded in an unpublished manuscript—"A Brahmin's Self-Laughter"—a mock-solemn chronicle full of the author's inimitable whim and fancy. The first authentic record of his ancestry, he crooned, could be found in the Book of Enoch, thirty-first chapter, which stated that "about this time (300 years before Adam) flourished Lowell of the Zarrows—a great king over much people." Adam's Eve, the chronicle went on, would not for a moment have hesitated to marry a Lowell, had the opportunity presented itself. That it hadn't was history's loss.

James Russell Lowell, proud of his heritage, merely intended in this burlesque to "lampoon the absurdities of ancestor-worship" and thereby deride the traditional and typical family history so common during this period—those vast genealogical tomes found today in almost every New England historical and antiquarian society.

Exercise 3-15

Try your hand at writing an opening to your story that uses unusual ideas.

_____

_____

_____

_____

_____

_____

_____

_____

_____

_____

_____

_____

The Baited Hook of Setting

A Cornish Childhood ends with the lights of Oxford—as they might be reflected in Mercury, the fountain-pool in Tom Quad, on the evening of my arrival, 11 October 1922. Every season has its particular beauty at Oxford, but I think of autumn as most characteristic of the place—the rich, ruddy colour of the creeper that covered Meadow Buildings, the plum-skin bloom of mist in the Meadows and about the quadrangles. Everywhere was the sound of bells: the deep reverberation of Great Tom that became so familiar, the hundred and one strokes at five past nine at night to call home the original number of students, the near-by sighing chime of the Cathedral bells from the squat Victorian tower, against the building of which Lewis Carroll levelled his pamphlet about the "meat-safe," with his portrait of the design - a perfect parallelogram. Across the Meadows to me in my room were blown the sound of innumerable other bells: the clack of solitary tintinnabulations of colleges calling their undergraduates to chapel or hall, the chimes of a city church, or loveliest of all, the full peal from Magdalen tower on May morning, that years later came to have a more affecting and personal connotation for me. If I had read Hopkins then, as I had not as yet, I might have had these among the many others in my head to express what I felt:

Towery city and branchy between towers;

Cuckoo-echoing, bell-swarméd, lark-charméd,

rock-racked, river-rounded . . .

— A.L. Rowse, *A Cornishman at Oxford*

We have the main character, we know the basic theme, his life at Oxford, and we certainly are aware of the setting.

Figure 3-16

Try writing an opening to your story by describing a setting.

_____

_____

_____

_____

_____

_____

_____

_____

_____

_____

_____

_____

_____

The Baited Hook of Action

Of all the openings, action is the preferred. Why? Because it moves us almost directly to that point at which we proceed along the road of resolving the basic problem of the narrative.

> They didn't say anything about this in the books, I thought, as the snow blew in through the gaping doorway and settled on my naked back.
>
> I lay face down on the cobbled floor in a pool of nameless muck, my arm deep inside the straining cow, my feet scrabbling for a toe hold between the stones. I was stripped to the waist and the snow mingled with the dirt and the dried blood on my body. I could see nothing outside the circle of flickering light thrown by the smoking oil lamp which the farmer held over me.
>
> No, there wasn't a word in the books about searching for your ropes and instruments in the shadows; about trying to keep clean in a half bucket of tepid water; about the cobbles digging into your chest. Nor about the slow numbing of the arms, the creeping paralysis of the muscles as the fingers tried to work against the cow's powerful expulsive efforts.
>
> — James Herriot, *All Creatures Great and Small*

Herriot's action opening drops us directly into the basic problem of his autobiography: his struggle as a veterinarian surgeon to keep animals healthy and productive in difficult and trying circumstances. We also know the main character, and we certainly know the setting.

Exercise 3-16

Try your hand at writing an opening that drops the reader directly into the action.

_____

_____

_____

_____

_____

_____

_____

_____

_____

STEP FIVE: TRANSITION BETWEEN SCENES

There is one final problem that we touched on in step 3 but have not considered in depth: stringing or linking scenes together. In *WFN* (104-107), a scene is defined as a division that advances the theme or conflict of the narrative; in addition, a scene usually has a limited set of people and takes place in a certain location at a certain time (see the discussion on the "French scene," *WFN*, 106). While the final scene in a novel or longer narrative brings together all the laments of the various scenes to resolve the basic conflict, the scenes building up to the final scene are steps or building blocks in advancing towards that ultimate resolution and must accordingly be organically related to the basic theme of the narrative. The problem is that there is no clear agreement as to what a scene is, and no scientific way of arriving at such a definition. Writers talk about transitional, expository, developmental, relief, forest, balcony, street, court, chamber, not to mention short and long scenes, and none seem able to agree as to what a scene exactly is.

The story in this workbook entitled "The Tunnel" and the prose version of William Grant's time in prison differ in length as well as in number of scenes: "The Tunnel" consists of one scene (a limited number of characters set in a certain location and time with a confrontation ending in a resolution); the narrative dealing with Grant's imprisonment consists of two basic scenes, although there are several transitional, expository, or developmental scenes. In the Grant narrative, then, both scenes, though set in different locations and at different times, must work together to resolve the basic conflict of the narrative.

Looking back now at the Grant narrative, most readers would agree that the two basic scenes are Grant's attendance of a Mormon general conference and his time in prison. Since I have treated the general conference scene as the main scene of the story, the time in prison becomes a flashback or painful memory. Both scenes are related, but they are not the same in time and place; and to aid in the presentation of these two basic scenes, I have employed several short transitional, expository, or developmental scenes whose purpose is to lead up to and away from the prison term and the conference in Salt Lake City and to relate the two scenes logically since I present them out of chronological sequence. If the primary function of the prison scene is to show Grant being defeated by the physical confinement of prison life, the arrest and sentencing scenes are transitional or developmental. Similarly, if I want to show the ultimate public shame and emotional destruction of the man in the forced Mormon retreat from polygamy, I have to get him to conference, and the train scene, with its tragic references to his son's drowning, is once again developmental because it leads us up to his final emotional destruction when he hears the famous "Manifesto."

Exercise 3-17

Turn to the detailed chapter outline you prepared in exercise 3-13; isolate the scenes within your chapter, keeping in mind that a chapter certainly could be one scene. Consider the following ways in which you might link two or more of these scenes. (Examples below are from the Grant narrative and relate to the two basic scenes and to various developmental, expository, or transitional scenes.) Choose transition strategies that will help you move your narrative from one scene to another; then write the scene.

LEAVE A BARRIER OF SPACE, AN EXTENDED BLANK, OR A NEW CHAPTER: A barrier of space separates the moment when the train rounds the Point of the Mountain, and the narrative shifts back in time to Grant's arrest for polygamy.

MAKE A SHIFT CHANGE IN TIME: "Then on Saturday morning . . .." "When he awoke the morning of his third day . . . ." "The gradual braking of the train brought William back into the present." "When he had been released, William . . . ."

_____

_____

_____

_____

_____

_____

_____

_____

_____

_____

MAKE A SHIFT IN LOCATION: "The prison house was built of brick" "It was dark when the train ground and clanked to a halt at the American Fork station."

_____

_____

_____

_____

_____

_____

_____

_____

_____

_____

USE TRANSITIONAL PHRASES: "After the service . . . ." "It took almost an hour to . . . ."

_____

_____

_____

USE NARRATIVE SUMMARY: "The prison house was built of brick and in the winter was heated by steam. But summer was now coming on and there was little that could be done to ward off its devastating heat."

_____

_____

_____

_____

USE A CHARACTER (dialogue, emotion, mood, or thought) TO ANNOUNCE A CHANGE:

Dialogue: ("What do you have to say?")

_____

_____

Emotion: ("Gathering courage and strength . . . .")

_____

_____

Mood: "But now reality began to set in."

_____

_____

Thought:"If he saw or passed anyone he knew, he was absolutely unaware."

_____

_____

Now write the several scenes that you have outlined, adding the transitions you feel will work best to bridge one scene to another.

STEP SIX: WRITING EFFECTIVE DIALOGUE

In step 1, Characterization, you were asked to observe and gather dialogue patterns for a certain character. If you have listened well and made adequate notes, you are now ready to weave dialogue into your narrative. In doing so, there are certain ground rules which most writers of narrative observe:

1.   Avoid the constant and excessive use of "he said/she said" tags particularly when it is obvious who the speaker is.

2.   Write natural and character-appropriate dialogue.

3.   Stagger and vary the placement of tags.

4.   Weave action and emotional reaction into tags.

5.   Include dialogue only if it has a purpose or contributes to the resolution of the basic problem of the story.

Writing effective dialogue into a narrative is, however, far more than observing a few basic rules. In fact, rule 1, avoiding the constant and excessive use of "he said/she said" tags is violated by many writers—and with a certain measure of success. However, one simply cannot help but wonder how much more effective the dialogue might have been had the authors attempted to utilize rules 2 through 5.

Note the following example of repetitious placement and kind of tag:

> My father and mother were up there a long time, enough time for the choir to go through four hymns and Comrades in Arms, and then I heard them coming down. Back they came to the kitchen again and they stood by the table.
>
> "Well, Gwilyhm," my mother said, and looking at him.
>
> "Well, Beth," said my father, and smiling.

"There is beautiful," said my mother.

"Glad I am you like it," my father said.

"What is left in the box, now?" my mother asked.

"Plenty, plenty, and to spare," said my father, still smiling and giving a wink to me.

— Llewellyn, *How Green Was My Valley*

Each writer should isolate and identify tag styles that he appreciates in other writers and employ or adapt the particular tag style that works well for him. The following quotes are examples of various tag styles.

Identifying Speakers Through Action Tags

My mother said, "You're going too fast for these turns."

"Look at the fog. Now isn't that nice?" He stuck his head out the window. "By gum, that was a possum. Mary, take a look." He maneuvered another switchback.

Mary said, "I don't see anything."

"Right in the crotch of that big tree." The car was going in one direction, and he was looking in the other.

Mother reached for the steering wheel, catching George on the chin. My father came back into the car and pushed her hand away. "The last time you did that," he said in a conversational tone, "we sideswiped a truck."

She was a pushover. "If I hadn't, we'd have hit it head-on. Isn't that so, children?"

Witnesses last autumn outside Atlanta, we were jurors now. We took our duties seriously. We nodded, for her to see, but remained quiet, for him not to hear.

— Packer, *In My Father's House*

Exercise 3-18

Choose a section from the narrative you are writing and present dialogue using action tags.

_____

_____

_____

_____

_____

_____

_____

_____

Staggering the Placement of Tags

Siegfried looked up, startled, from his soup. "What in God's name is that?"

"Must be that dog I operated on this morning," I replied. "The odd one does that coming out of barbiturates. I expect he'll stop soon."

Siegfried looked at me doubtfully. "Well, I hope so—I could soon get tired of that. Gives me the creeps."

— James Herriot, *All Creatures Great and Small*

Exercise 3-19

Choose a section from the narrative you are writing and present dialogue, staggering the placement of tags.

_____

_____

_____

_____

_____

_____

_____

_____

Weaving Emotional Reaction Into Tags

"What's wrong with me, Allie?" he would ask as he fell into bed exhausted night after night.

The answer was always the same. "Bill, you're working too hard. You're trying to do too much."

"I know, that's what the doctors tell me. Maybe they're right." Then, already half-gone, "Allie, could we get away for awhile—go out to Utah—go riding—see the mountains—?"

Before Allie could answer, he'd sink into sleep like a man falling into the sea.

— Robert O'Brien, *Marriott*

Exercise 3-20

Choose a section from the narrative you are writing and present dialogue while weaving emotional reaction into your tags.

_____

_____

_____

_____

_____

_____

_____

_____

Interspersing Direct Quotes With Indirect Quotations.

This kind of tag style works well with an autobiography or in writing a narrative based on a journal. It is a good device to use when you know only part of a conversation or have only a limited number of quotes at your disposal.

"That won't do at all, James. I'll have a word with Hammond about it. Leave it with me."

And then a few days later when I made a further appeal.

"Oh Lord, yes. I've been meaning to fix it up with Hammond. Don't worry, James, I'll see to it."

Finally I had to tell him that when I put my foot on the pedal there was nothing at all and the only way I had of stopping the car was to crash it into bottom gear.

"Oh bad luck, James. Must be a nuisance for you. But never mind, I'll arrange everything."

Some time later I asked Mr. Hammond down at the garage if he had heard anything from Siegfried, but he hadn't.

— James Herriot, *All Creatures Great and Small*

Exercise 3-21

Choose a section from the narrative you are writing and present dialogue, interspersing direct quotes with indirect quotations.

_____

_____

_____

_____

_____

_____

_____

_____

Interjecting Dialogue Into Extensive Narrative and Commentary

This tag style also serves the purposes of the family narrative. It weaves dialogue highlights into the narrative fabric, allowing the writer to construct the kind of document typical of many family histories.

> When I asked at the shop for "gurts" the supercilious young woman affected not to know what I wanted, and at last as a great concession suggested, "Oh, it's groats you mean.' My reaction was a very active one: shame, humiliation, indignation with the young woman and a rising tide of anger with the stupidity at home which was responsible for the humiliation. Tears of vexation burned in my eyes all the way up the road, and arriving with the precious packet I threw it on the table, adding: "And if you want to know," (this very cuttingly) "it's not called gurts, but **groats**"—and flung out . . . .

> — A.L.Rowse, *A Cornish Childhood*

Another example of this technique:

> We all got ready for church. As was her usual practice, Mama checked each of us in turn: a collar adjusted here, hair pulled back there, a soft caress for each.

> It was my turn last. She set her very large brown eyes on mine. "Felice," she said, "do you understand why the Christmas Angel couldn't leave you gifts?"

> "Uh-huh," I answered.

> "The Angel reminds us that we will always get what we deserve. We can't escape it. Sometimes it's hard to understand and it hurts and makes us cry. But it teaches us what's right and wrong, and we get better every year."

> I'm not certain that at the time I really understood what she meant. I knew only that I was sure I was loved, that whatever I had done, I had been forgiven, and that there always would be another chance for me.

> I have never forgotten that Christmas so many years ago. Since then life has not always been fair or offered me what I thought I'd deserved or rewarded my being good. Over the years I know that I have been selfish, bratty, thoughtless, and perhaps, at times, even cruel . . . but I have never forgotten that where there is forgiveness, sharing, another chance given, and unwavering love, the Christmas Angel is always present and it's always Christmas.

> — Leo Buscaglia, *Seven Stories of Christmas Love*

Exercise 3-22

Choose a section from the narrative you are writing and present dialogue, interjecting occasional dialogue into extensive narrative and commentary.

_____

_____

_____

_____

_____

_____

_____

_____

_____

_____

_____

_____

_____

_____

_____

_____

_____

_____

_____

CHAPTER 4

ORIENTING THE STORY

PERSPECTIVE, TIME AND PLACE, AND PERSON

STEP ONE: READ EXTENSIVELY IN BACKGROUND MATERIALS

The first step in orienting the story is to gain historical perspective or understanding about a certain period by developing a reliable period bibliography. This takes time, and it must be done well; if not, you will never accurately understand the person or the family about which you are writing.

Any time a writer characterizes a person or members of a family, he can hardly avoid considering the historical period in which the person or the family lived. While we were constantly aware of the historical period as we developed the concept of characterization in chapter 2, we need now to look more carefully beyond the particular person or family to see how that person or members of that family fit into or distinguished themselves from other individuals in a specific historical period. The focus in chapter 2 was how a particular person or persons behaved, thought, and felt. Our task now is to isolate broader themes, to understand how people generally behaved, thought, and felt during a particular historical period, so that we can check the accuracy of our characterization or characterizations against the historical context and see that person or persons as a reflection as well as a contradiction of the historical context.

The following publications, particularly the five books in the History-of-Private-Life series, contain extensive bibliographies. University publishers also periodically send out lists of current publications. Unfortunately, university publishers publish across state and national boundaries, so you cannot be certain that once you have considered all the publications from a particular state university that you have seen all the titles currently being published on that state.

General Period Publications

Ariès, Philippe and Georges Duby. *A History of Private Life*. Vol. 1, *From Pagan Rome to Byzantium*. Cambridge, Mass.: Belknap Press of Harvard University Press, 1987. This book, which focuses on Europe, reveals what it was like to live, work, and die in the ancient world. The book contains an excellent bibliography with several hundred references for further reading.

———. *A History of Private Life*. Vol. 2, *Revelations of the Medieval World*. Cambridge, Mass.: Belknap Press of Harvard University Press, 1988. This volume explores the evolving concepts of intimacy from the semiobscure eleventh century through the first hints of the Renaissance world.

———. A History of Private Life. Vol. 3, *Passions of the Renaissance*. Cambridge, Mass.: Belknap Press of Harvard University Press, 1989.This volume celebrates the emergence of individualism in ordinary and extraordinary people.

Perrot, Michelle. *A History of Private Life*. Vol. 4, *From the Fires of Revolution to the Great War*. Cambridge, Mass.: Belknap Press of Harvard University Press, 1988. This volume addresses the golden age of private life with its affirmation of the common man.

Prost, Antoine and Gérard Vincent. *A History of Private Life*. Vol. 5, *Riddles of Identity in Modern Times*. Cambridge, Mass.: Belknap Press of Harvard University Press, 1991. This volume charts the flowering of personal identity in the period following World War I. It draws on many sources, both familiar and unfamiliar to the family historian.

Fischer, David Hackett. *Albion's Seed: Four British Folkways in America*. New York: Oxford University Press, 1989. This book is the first in a projected series of five that will eventually comprise the cultural history of the United States. *Albion's Seed* takes up the problem of the cultural origins of the United States. In the author's words, this book is "about change and continuity in the acts and thoughts of ordinary people." No book offers a better point of departure for understanding one's ancestors.

Strauss, William and Neil Howe. *The History of America's Future 1584 to 2069*. New York: William Morrow and Company, Inc., 1991. While the authors make assertions that sometimes strike the reader as premature and simplistic, they still provide a useful set of analytical tools. Their thesis is that each generation exhibits a distinctive pattern and that all the various patterns can be reduced to four basic types that repeat themselves sequentially. For the family historian writing about an American family, they provide a useful starting point.

Hard-to-find and Out-of-print Family and Local Histories

There are several bibliographies and companies that print catalogs of hard-to-find, out-of-print family and local histories.

Schreiner-Yantis, Netti. *Genealogical and Local History Books in Print*. Springfield, Virg.: Genealogical Books in Print, 1985.

Goodspeed's Bookshop, Inc., Dept. NE, 7 Beacon St.,Boston, MA 02108; (617) 523-5970. Ask for the catalog *Goodspeed's Catalogue of Genealogies and Local History*.

Higginson Book Co., 14 Derby Square, Salem, MA 01970; (508) 853-6015.

University Microfilms International, Research Collections Information Service, 300 North Zeeb Road, Ann Arbor, MI 48106-1346. Ask for the catalog *Family Histories for Genealogists*.

Tuttle Antiquarian Books, Inc., P.O. Box 541, Rutland, VT 05701-0541; (802) 773-8229. Ask for the catalog *Genealogy, Local History, and Heraldry*.

Popular Magazines

Reminisce: The Magazine That Brings Back the Good Times. Greendale, WI: Reiman Publications.

Good Old Days. Des Moines, Iowa: The House of White Birches, Inc.

University Publishers

There are several university presses that specialize in family and local histories that explore the background of a particular state or region. Occasionally, you will find a university publisher in one state publishing a book or a journal about another state or region. If you are on these publishers' mailing lists, normally you should receive periodical listings of current publications. For other publishers that deal with your area of interest, check *Publishers' Directory* for lists of publishers organized by region. (*Publishers' Directory* is an annual published by Gale Research Inc. and is available in most libraries.)

Universite de Moncton, Centre d'Etudes Acadiennes, Moncton, NB, Canada E1A 3E9

Universite de Montreal, Presses de l'Universite de Montreal, CP 6128, Suc A, Montreal, PQ, Canada H3C 3J7

Universite du Quebec, Presses de l'Universite du Quebec, 2875 boul Laurier, Suite Foy, PQ, Canada G1V 2M3

University College of Cape Breton Press, P.O. Box 5300, Sydney, NS, Canada B1P 6L2

University of Alabama, Tuscaloosa, University of Alabama Press, PO Box 870380, Tuscaloosa, AL 35487

University of Alaska, Fairbanks University of Alaska Press, Gruening Building, Fairbanks, AK 99775-1580

University of Alberta, Canadian Institute of Ukrainian Studies Press, 352 Athabasca Hall, Edmonton, AB, Canada T6G 2E8

University of Alberta, Department of Geography, Edmonton, AB, Canada T6G 2H4

University of Arizona, Tucson, University of Arizona Press, 1230 North Park Avenue, Suite 102, Tucson, AZ 85719

University of Arkansas, Fayetteville, University of Arkansas Press, Fayetteville, AR 72701

University of California, Berkeley, University of California Press, 2120 Berkeley Way, Berkeley, CA 94720

University of Central Arkansas, University of Central Arkansas Press, P.O. Box 4933, Conway, AR 72032

University of Charleston, Mountain State Press, 2300 MacCorkle Avenue, SE, Charleston, WV 25304

University of Chicago, University of Chicago Press, 5801 Ellis Avenue, Chicago, IL 60637

University of Colorado, Colorado Springs Writers' Forum, Colorado Springs, CO 80933-7150

University of Georgia, Athens, University of Georgia Press, Terrel Hall, Athens, GA 30602

University of Hawaii, Honolulu, University of Hawaii Press, 2840 Kolowalu Street, Honolulu, HI 96822

University of Idaho, Moscow, University of Idaho Press, Moscow, ID 83843

University of Illinois, Urbana-Champaign, University of Illinois Press, 54 East Gregory Drive, Champaign IL 61820

University of Iowa, Iowa City, University of Iowa Press, 119 West Park Road, Iowa City, IA 52242

University of Kansas, Lawrence, University of Kansas Press, Lawrence, KS 66049

University of Kentucky, Lexington, King Library Press, Special Collections and Archives, Lexington, KY 40506-0039

University of Kentucky, Lexington, University Press of Kentucky, 663 South Limestone Street, Lexington, KY 40506-0336

University of Lowell, Lowell Conference on Industrial History, 171 Merrimack Street, Lowell, MA 01852

University of Maine, Orono, University of Maine Press, 51 PICS Building, Orono, ME 04469

University of Massachusetts, Amherst, University of Massachusetts Press, P.O. Box 429, Amherst, MA 01004

University of Mississippi, Jackson, University Press of Mississippi, 3825 Ridgewood Road, Jackson, MS 39211

University of Mississippi, University, Center for the Study of Southern Culture, Barnard Observatory, University, MS 38677

University of Missouri, Columbia, University of Missouri Press, 2910 LeMone Blvd., Columbia, MO 65201

University of Nebraska, Lincoln, University of Nebraska Press, 901 North 17th Street, Lincoln, NE 68588-0520

University of Nevada, Reno, University of Nevada Press, Reno, NV 89507-0076

University of New Brunswick, Acadiensis Press, Campus House, P.O. Box 4400, Fredericton, NB, Canada E3B 5A3

University of New Brunswick, Micmac-Maliseet Institute, Fredericton, NB, Canada E3B 6E3

University of New Mexico, Albuquerque, University of New Mexico Press, 1720 Lomas Blvd. NE, Albuquerque, NM 87131-1591

University of North Carolina, Chapel Hill, University of North Carolina Press, 116 South Boundary Street, P.O. Box 2288, Chapel Hill, NC 27515-2288

University of North Texas, University of North Texas Press, P.O. Box 13856, Denton, TX 76203

University of Oklahoma, Norman, University of Oklahoma Press, 1005 Asp Avenue, Norman, OK 73109

University of Pennsylvania, Philadelphia, University of Pennsylvania Press, Blockley Hall, 418 Service Drive, Philadephia, PA 19104

University of Pittsburgh, University of Pittsburgh Press, 127 North Bellefield Avenue, Pittsburgh, PA 15260

University of Portland, University of Portland Press, 5000 North Willamette Blvd., Portland, OR 97203

University of Puerto Rico, Rio Piedras University of Puerto Rico Press/Editorial de la Universidad de Puerto Rico, Box 23322, UPR Station, Rio Piedras, PR 00931

University of Regina, Canadian Plains Research Center, Regina, SK, Canada S4S OA2

University of Regina, Department of Geography, Regina, SK, Canada S4S OA2

University of South Carolina, Columbia, University of South Carolina Press, Columbia, SC 29208

University of South Dakota, Vermillion, University of South Dakota Press, Vermillion, SD 57069-2390

University of Tennessee, Knoxville, University of Tennessee Press, 293 Communications Building, Knoxville, TN 37996

University of Texas, Austin, Center for Mexican American Studies, Student Service Building, Austin, TX 78712

University of Texas, Austin Institute of Texan Cultures at San Antonio, P.O. Box 1226, San Antonio, TX 78294-1226

University of Utah, Salt Lake City, Annie Clark Tanner Trust Fund, Library, Salt Lake City, UT 84112

University of Utah, Salt Lake City, University of Utah Press, 101 U.U.P., Salt Lake City, UT 84112

University of Victoria, Western Geographical Series, Department of Geography, P.O. Box 1700, Victoria, BC, Canada V8W 2Y2

University of Virginia, Charlottesville, University Press of Virginia, P.O. Box 3608, University Station, Charlottesville, VA

University of Wyoming, Laramie, U.W. Publication, P.O. Box 3315, University Station, Laramie, WY 82071

University Press of Colorado, P.O. Box 849, Niwot, CO 80544

University Press of New England, 17 1/2 Lebanon Street, Hanover, NH 03755

Utah Division of State History/Utah State Historical Society, 300 Rio Grande, Salt Lake City, UT 84101

Utah State University, Utah State University Press, Logan, UT 84322-7800

Consider the books you gather, particularly their bibliographies as well as the bibliographies at the end of *WFN* chapter 2, and develop a specialized bibliography that focuses on the time and place of your family of interest. This is an ongoing process, one that you will never complete or certainly never be satisfied with. Spend some time each day reading and adding to or deleting from your specialized bibliography as you explore for other pertinent books.

STEP TWO: ANALYZE AND INTERPRET LANDSCAPES, BUILDINGS, PICTURES, AND ARTIFACTS

The following selected bibliographies represent a sampling of what is being written in the area of material cultural analysis. For more complete bibliographies, consult W.G. Hoskins' *Local History in England* and David E. Kyvig and Myron A. Marty's *Nearby History: Exploring the Past Around You* as well as bibliographies in the titles listed below.

Analyzing Antiques

Boger, Louise A. and H. Batterson Boger, comps. and eds. *The Dictionary of Antiques and the Decorative Arts: A Book of References for Glass, Furniture, Ceramics, Silver, Periods, Styles, Technical Terms, Etc.* New York: Scribner's, 1957.

Coles, Ann Kilborn. *Antiques: How to Identify, Buy, Sell, Refinish, and Care for Them.* New York: David McKay, 1957.

Haywood, Helen, ed. *The Connoisseur's Handbook of Antique Collecting: A Dictionary of Furniture, Silver, Ceramics, Glass, Fine Arts, Etc.* London: Connoisseur, 1960.

Kirk, John T. *The Impecunious Collector's Guide to American Antiques.* New York: Knopf, 1975.

Analyzing Architectural Styles

Poppeliers, John, Chambers, S. Allen, and Nancy B. Schwartz. *What Style Is It?* Washington, D.C.: Preservation Press, 1977.

Whitten, Marcus. *American Architecture since 1780: A Guide to Styles.* Cambridge, Mass.: MIT Press, 1969.

Analyzing Artifacts

Ames, Kenneth. "Material Culture as Non-Verbal Communication: A Historical Case Study," *Journal of American Culture* 3 (1980): 619-641.

Ames, Kenneth and Gerald W.R. Ward, eds. *Decorative Arts and Household Furnishings in America, 1650-1920: An Annotated Bibliography.* Charlottesville, Virg.: University Press of Virginia, 1989.

Bailey, Lynn R. *From Adze to Vermilion: A Guide to the Hardware of History, and the Literature of Historic Sites Archeology.* Pasadena, Calif.: Socio-Technical Books, 1971.

Butler, Patrick H., III. *Material Culture as a Resource in Local History.* Chicago: Newberry Library, 1979.

Chavis, John. "The Artifact and the Study of History," *Curator* 7, no. 2 (1964): 156-162.

Kubler, *The Shape of Time: Remarks on the History of Things.* New Haven: Yale University Press, 1962.

Quimby, Ian M., ed. *Material Culture and the Study of American Life.* New York: W.W. Norton & Company, Inc., 1978.

St. George, Robert Blair, ed. *Material Life in America, 1600-1860.* Boston: Northeastern University Press, 1988.

Schlereth, Thomas. *Artifacts and the American Past.* Nashville, Tenn.: American Association for State and Local History, 1980.

—————. Cultural History and Material Culture: Everyday Life, Landscapes, Museums. Ann Arbor, Mich.: UMI Research Press, 1990.

Skramstad, Harold. "American Things: A Neglected Material Culture," *American Studies: An International Newsletter* 10, no. 3 (spring 1972): 11-22.

Schlebecker, John T. "The Use of Objects in Voice of the Artifact," *Agricultural History* 27 (1964): 245-50.

Analyzing Houses

Hart, John Fraser. *The Look of the Land.* Englewood Cliffs, N.J.: Prentice-Hall, 1975.

Rapoport, Amos. *House Form and Culture.* Englewood Cliffs, N.J.: Prentice-Hall, 1969.

Richert, John E. "House Facades of the Northeastern United States: A Tool of Geographic Analysis," *Annals*, Association of American Geographers, 57 (1967): 211-38.

Analyzing Photographs

Akeret, Robert U. *Photoanalysis.* New York: P.H. Wyden, 1973.

Bayer, Jonathan. *Reading Photographs: Understanding the Aesthetics of Photography.* New York: Pantheon, 1977.

Davies, Thomas L. *Shoots: A Guide to Your Family's Photographic Heritage.* Danbury, H.H.: Addison House, 1977.

Ford, Colin and Roy Strong. *An Early Victorian Album: The Hill/Adamson Collection.* London: Jonathan Cape, 1974.

Frisch-Ripley, Karen. *Unlocking the Secrets of Old Photographs.* Salt Lake City: Ancestry, 1991.

Peters, Marsha and Bernard Mergen. "Doing the Rest: The Uses of Photographs in American Studies," *American Quarterly* 29, no. 3 (1977): 280-303

Szarkowski, John. *Looking at Photographs: 100 Pictures from the Collection of the Museum of Modern Art.* New York: Museum of Modern Art, 1973.

—————. *The Photographer's Eye.* New York: Museum of Modern Art, 1966.

Analyzing Streets and Their Adornments

Rapoport, Amos. *History and Precedent in Environmental Design.* New York: Plenum Press, 1990.

Rifkind, Carole. *Main Street: The Face of Urban America.* New York: Harper and Row, 1977.

Rudofsky, Bernard. *Streets for People: A Primer for Americans.* Garden City, N.Y.: Doubleday, 1969.

Robert, *Street Art.* New York: Links, 1975.

STEP THREE: WRITE HISTORICAL SCRIPTS

Now that you have compiled a background bibliography and read several of these books, your task is to prepare an historical script setting forth generally what it meant to live in a certain historical period. In "Step One: Characterization" of chapter 3 of this workbook, you were directed in how to develop an accurate characterization of a real person who lived at a certain time and in a certain place. Now we are at the point at which we must check the accuracy of that characterization against the general historical script that a person living at that same time and in that same place might probably have followed. Where we had a specific historical person or persons in mind before, now we have a general type in mind. And as we look now at what a person living at that time in that place might have been expected to feel, think, and do, we may want to reconsider any specific characterizations.

First we must establish basic character information so that we can identify exactly what kind of an individual we are scripting. Men differed from women, those who lived in cities differed from those who worked on farms, and people differed in religious and patriotic values from national group to national group. Once we have settled basic questions such as gender, class, nationality, education, religion, and occupation, we can turn to more specific items in a script.

Exercise 4-1

Briefly answer the following questions:

What was my gender? _____

What were my physical characteristics? _____

_____

_____

What kinds of diseases, accidents, or tragedies did I have? _____

_____

_____

_____

_____

When did I live? _____

What national and international events occurred during my life? _____

_____

_____

_____

Where did I live? _____

_____

What kind of a house did I have? _____

_____

_____

What kind of a town, city, or village did I live in? _____

_____

_____

_____

What was my religion? _____

_____

What was my class in society? _____

_____

_____

What were my ambitions? _____

_____

_____

_____

What was my education? _____

_____

_____

What was my occupation? _____

_____

_____

What were my morals or values? _____

_____

_____

Was I married, divorced, or single? _____

_____

_____

How many children did I have? _____

Now that you have established the kind or type of individual that lived at a certain historical place and time, answer in short paragraphs the following questions, writing as if you were the hypothetical type whose perspective you are attempting to discover. Remember that it is impossible to distinguish clearly between what a person does, feels, or thinks; many of the questions in one category will overlap and duplicate ideas from other categories as well as overlap and duplicate questions in the same category. Further, as you write these short paragraphs, other questions or directions may occur to you that will be far more pertinent than the question you are addressing. So do not slavishly answer a question when you are convinced that another question or direction would give you a better feel for the type of person you are seeking to describe.

HOW WOULD I HAVE BEHAVED OR ACTED?

What would I have done routinely each day? _____

_____

_____

_____

_____

_____

What would have been some of my favorite expressions? _____

_____

_____

_____

_____

_____

What would have been my distinguishing habits? _____

_____

_____

_____

_____

_____

What kinds of foods would I have liked to eat? Drinks to drink? _____

_____

_____

_____

_____

_____

How would I have dressed? _____

_____

_____

_____

_____

_____

What kind of an education or training would I have had? _____

_____

_____

_____

_____

_____

What kinds of recognition or awards would I have sought? _____

_____

_____

_____

_____

_____

How would I have earned money? _____

_____

_____

_____

_____

_____

What did I do each day as worker, wife, mother, husband, or father? _____

_____

_____

_____

_____

_____

What would I have done with my money? How would I have shared it? _____

_____

_____

_____

_____

What kind of a house would I have lived in?_____

_____

_____

_____

_____

How would each room have been furnished? _____

_____

_____

_____

_____

What would I have done in each of the rooms of the house? _____

_____

_____

_____

_____

_____

How did people use space in the house—for working, sleeping, eating, living?_____

_____

_____

_____

_____

_____

How would the members of my family have shared sorrow, joy?_____

_____

_____

_____

_____

_____

How would I have related to my siblings?_____

_____

_____

_____

_____

What kind of care would I have provided the sick, the aged?_____

_____

_____

_____

_____

What was I expected to do as a child, a spouse, a parent? _____

_____

_____

_____

_____

_____

How would I have been expected to act as an older person? _____

_____

_____

_____

_____

_____

How would I have raised children? _____

_____

_____

_____

_____

What would I have done for pleasure, leisure? _____

_____

_____

_____

_____

_____

What kinds of festivities and celebrations, entertainment, dances, family outings, and games would I have participated in?_____

_____

_____

_____

_____

What kinds of pets would I have had? _____

_____

_____

_____

_____

_____

What would have been my military obligations as a male? _____

_____

_____

_____

_____

_____

What would have been unusual for me to do, but which I might well have done? _____

_____

_____

_____

_____

_____

What would have been difficult for me to do? _____

_____

_____

_____

_____

_____

HOW WOULD I HAVE FELT?

What would I have liked most about myself? Least? _____

_____

_____

_____

_____

What would have embarrassed me?_____

_____

_____

_____

_____

What were my special interests and desires?_____

_____

_____

_____

_____

What would have been my most pressing problem or caused me deep anxiety? _____

_____

_____

_____

_____

_____

What would have been my greatest hopes or would have made me happy? _____

_____

_____

_____

_____

_____

What would I have felt my role to be as a man? As a woman? _____

_____

_____

_____

_____

_____

What would have been bad luck? Good luck? Magic? _____

_____

_____

_____

_____

What would my parents have said to me when they were pleased with me? _____

_____

_____

_____

_____

_____

How would I have fallen in love and courted? _____

_____

_____

_____

_____

What would I have felt and said when I was angry with a member of the opposite sex? Pleased? _____

_____

_____

_____

_____

How would I have felt about my parents, my siblings, in-laws, and relatives? _____

_____

_____

_____

_____

What would have been my feelings about other religions or racial groups? _____

_____

_____

_____

_____

What would have been my feelings and attitudes about governments, kings, or national leaders?_____

_____

_____

_____

_____

How did war or wars affect my life? _____

_____

_____

_____

_____

How would I have dealt with calamity or death, tragedy or sorrow? _____

_____

_____

_____

_____

_____

What kind of poetry and music would I have liked? _____

_____

_____

_____

_____

_____

What kinds of songs would I have sung? _____

_____

_____

_____

_____

_____

What kind of art would have hung in my house? _____

_____

_____

_____

_____

What kinds of stories would I have listened to and liked? _____

_____

_____

_____

_____

_____

HOW WOULD I HAVE THOUGHT?

What would my parents have said to me when they were angry with me? _____

_____

_____

_____

_____

_____

What would my parents have told me about my birth? _____

_____

_____

_____

_____

_____

What would have been the main advice that my father would have given me? My mother? _____

_____

_____

_____

_____

_____

What would I have thought a man's role would be? A woman's role? _____

_____

_____

_____

_____

_____

Who would have been my hero or heros? _____

_____

_____

_____

_____

_____

How would I have described myself? _____

_____

_____

_____

_____

What would I have read? _____

_____

_____

_____

_____

_____

How would I have conceptualized tragedy and happiness? _____

_____

_____

_____

_____

If I could have made everything go right in my life, what would I have become? _____

_____

_____

_____

_____

What would I have wanted to learn in my life? _____

_____

_____

_____

_____

What would I have thought to be a wise use of time? A waste of time? _____

_____

_____

_____

_____

_____

What would I have thought about my community, my country, other nations? _____

_____

_____

_____

_____

How would I have described those about me? _____

_____

_____

_____

_____

What would I have thought of older people? Of younger people? My father? My mother? My brothers and sisters? My children? _____

_____

_____

_____

_____

What would I have thought of the rich and powerful? The poor and powerless? _____

_____

_____

STEP FOUR: RECREATE THE TIME AND PLACE

Now that you have a fairly good idea of the peculiar perspective of your historical subject or subjects, it is time to reconstruct the historical time and place.

In Henrik Ibsen's play *Peer Gynt*, the strange, irrepressible Norwegian hero Peer leaves his mother Åse on the roof of one of her farm buildings, the mill roof to be exact. The scene was to me totally incomprehensible until I quite by chance visited the Seurasaari Open-Air Museum outside Helsinki. This museum was founded in 1909 by a Professor Heikel, whose goal it was to collect typical buildings from the different regions of Finland to demonstrate how Finnish people had lived and worked. Finland is not Norway, but the architecture is similar. The late eighteenth-century Niemelä tenant farm from central Finland is composed of a main dwelling with several other, smaller buildings, all low enough that a reasonably strong man could have easily lifted his mother directly onto one of its roofs. It was not until I saw an actual Scandinavian farm that I really understood Ibsen's play.

For years now I have become familiar with many of these living museums, particularly those that illustrate areas of the world from which my various ancestral families hailed. The Kentish "rup" or "up" ending of my paternal surname could well imply Danish ancestry; so when I visited York, England, the capital of ancient Danelaw, I toured the Jorvik Viking Centre. Many of my mother's lines came from Bas-Rhin, France, the area we know as Alsace. They were weavers, and it was my visit to Das Elsässisches Museum in Strassbourg that first brought me to understand how people worked and lived in the same close quarters. The thatched and whitewashed cottages in the Welsh Folk Museum at St. Fagans just outside Cardiff, Wales, also helped me to understand how my Welsh ancestors had lived in an area no bigger than the two rooms of a modern house. This remarkable living museum exhibits every feature of Welsh life from utensils to complete buildings, and it literally brings to life the vague references made in historical accounts.

The family historian should take advantage of the remarkable living museums now common and popular in North and South America as well as in Western Europe. Almost every county and major town has one if not several, and they all provide quick and easy understanding of setting, time, and place. If you cannot visit these areas, you might consider writing some of these museums for illustrative publications. Nothing, however, will adequately substitute for the experience of visiting the actual places where your ancestors lived and worked. Some publications that list these museum villages follow:

Adams, Richard et. al. *Book of British Villages*. Basingstoke, Hants, England: Drive Publications Limited for the Automobile Association, 1983.

Allegre, Mitchell R. *A Guide to Museum Villages: The American Heritage Brought to Life*. New York: Arco, 1978.

Gutek, Gerald and Patricia Gutek. *Experiencing America's Past: A Travel Guide to Museum Villages.* New York: John Wiley and Sons, Inc., 1986.

Haas, Irvin. *America's Historic Villages and Restorations.* New York: Arco Publishing, 1974.

Restored Village Directory: *An Illustrated Directory Listing of Restored, Recreated and Replica Villages of Historic Interest in the United States and Canada.* 3d ed. New York: Quadrant Press, 1973.

Zook, Nicholas. *Museum Villages, U.S.A.* Barre, Mass.: Barre, 1971.

Exercise 4-2

In writing, it is important that you capture all of the elements of the setting. Indicate below those elements that make up the setting of your story; be certain to include most if not all of these elements, at least indirectly. It is, of course, assumed that you limit your descriptions to the time period of your story. Do not forget to include in your descriptions the physical descriptions as well as the atmosphere that each element or object evokes. For now, simply make a list of the items that would explain each element:

The general landscape (race, language, economy, area name[s], rivers, hills, transportation, roads, railways)_____

_____

_____

_____

_____

_____

_____

The season of the story and seasonal variations of the area (temperatures, rain, snow, wind, fog)_____

_____

_____

_____

_____

_____

_____

_____

The town or village (limits of town or village, churches, shops and stores, schools, health facilities, taverns, theaters, fraternal halls, government and police facilities) _____

_____

_____

_____

_____

_____

_____

The quarter in which the family home was placed (streets, trees, parks and open spaces, porches and balconies, gardens)_____

_____

_____

_____

_____

_____

_____

The construction and exterior of the family home as well as its outbuildings and implements (when built, designer, builder, architectural style, dimensions, number of rooms, stables, barns, mills, granaries, remodeling, expansion) _____

_____

_____

_____

_____

_____

_____

The floor plan and layout of the home with a functional description of each room or area (number of rooms, bedrooms, closets, sitting-rooms, attic, garages, pantry, porches, balconies, studies, kitchens, dairies, fireplaces, heating)_____

_____

_____

_____

_____

_____

The furnishings, utensils, foods, and decorations of the home (furniture, kitchen equipment, wallpaper, lighting, pictures, and paintings) _____

_____

_____

_____

_____

_____

The workplaces (implements, shops, mills, home work areas, canals, products, animals) _____

_____

_____

_____

_____

_____

STEP FIVE: DE-CENTER YOUR EXPOSITION AND NARRATIVE

Check your writing at all times to determine if you have sufficiently distanced yourself from what you have written. We have all seen movies and read stories and books set in the so-called historical past that are thinly disguised representations of the here and now. The point to remember here is that if you are writing a family history which you have not personally experienced, you should move yourself as far as possible from your story and allow the characters and the plot to speak for themselves. In other words, you should "de-center" or take yourself out of the center of what you are writing.

Lucy Maud Montgomery, author of the Anne-of-Green-Gables novels, is a good example of this problem. One only has to read a couple of novels beyond her first, *Anne of Green Gables*, to realize how much she repeats basic ideas and problems. Why? Because no matter what she wrote she really was telling only one story: her own. *The Selected Journals of L.M. Montgomery* dramatically demonstrate that everything she wrote sprang from her personal experience and life; she had lived it all before she had written it down. No one would or could argue that it did not work for her; after all, she made no attempt to pass her stories off as stories about life on Prince Edward Island a century before she had lived. And her novels were and are immensely popular.

The challenge for the family writer is the constant temptation to write himself or herself into the story. Everything we have discussed in this chapter so far makes the same point over and over: your dreams, your problems, your frustrations, and your successes were not necessarily the dreams, problems, frustrations, and successes of those who lived before you. You are not the center of what you are writing. Check over and over again to determine that you are striving to reveal the historical mindset of the person about whom you are writing.

STEP SIX: CHOOSE THE CORRECT PERSON AND POINT OF VIEW

The final issue in orienting a story is the question of person. Of the three ingredients—perspective, time and place, and person—person allows the most choice but also demands the most technical virtuosity.

Consider the following. One day you were travelling through a deep forest in a far-off country when you came across a clearing, in the center of which stood a snug little house. Curious that you should find a house in such a lonely place, you crept up to one of the windows where you witnessed a small, lively girl with a profusion of silver locks systematically tasting cooling porridge from three bowls: a great, deep bowl; a middle-size bowl; and a small, shallow bowl. As you watched, she settled on the small bowl, devouring its contents. Her hunger now satisfied, she marched boldly into the parlor, where she tried sitting alternately in three chairs, ultimately breaking out the bottom of the smallest one and falling with a bump to the ground. Upset and a bit bruised, she then went into the bedroom, and while it was a little difficult for you to make out what she was doing from your vantage point at the window, she seemed to try out each bed, settling on one and falling fast asleep.

As she slept peacefully, oblivious to danger, you were suddenly startled by three bears who, lumbering out of the dense forest dressed in the native costumes of the region and upright on their hind legs, opened the door to the house. Taking long looks at the disturbed porridge bowls on the table, they began to roar. While you had little idea what the bears were saying since they were speaking both in a foreign language as well as in bear talk, you observed that they were very upset. Their confusion and anger seemed to mount when they saw the broken chair and the disturbed beds. The three bears began to argue vehemently, and you became convinced that the two larger bears were intent on eating the small girl with silver locks. The small bear, however, seemed to be protecting the girl, making motions as if he wanted only to kiss her and send her on her way. While they continued roaring and arguing and moving in a confusing pattern around and between the beds, the little girl, by now awake and realizing that she was in real danger, slipped out of the bed, jumped quickly through the open window, and ran off into the dense forest as fast as she could. Fearful that you might well be the next subject for dinner, you decided that this was also a good time for you to return to town.

Upon arriving back home, you decided to tell this story to your friends. On the first telling, you probably simply related what you saw as you watched from the window. You were first mildly interested, then concerned for the young girl, and finally frightened out of your wits; and since you told the story as you saw it unfold before your eyes, in the first person, your observations were limited by your obstructed vantage point at the window, which did not allow you to see directly into the bedroom, by the fact that you did not understand the local dialect as well as bear talk, and finally by your sudden flight from the scene when the roaring and arguing drove the little girl out the bedroom window. This would be first person limited.

As time progressed, you found yourself being asked to repeat this story to local church and civic groups. In fact, the story was making you somewhat of a curiosity. So you began to do some library research, ask questions of bear experts and consult people who had travelled often to this foreign land. And as you gained more understanding, you began to tell the story not as you observed it but interpreting events with references to psychology, animal behavior, and foreign custom. Now removing yourself from the action of the story, you reported in the third person the young girl's actions and her thoughts and her fears, then the bears' frustration on coming home to no porridge and finding their comfortable home violated, finally ending with some observations on the habits of bears in a world wrecked by ecological disasters perpetuated by unthinking human beings. This would be third person omniscient.

The story continued to arouse widespread interest, and you found yourself being pulled between the interests of different groups. Social workers who were concerned with the potential of child abuse were never completely satisfied when you began to refer to the ecological rights of the bears, and environmentalists were distressed when you seemed to be taken with the lively little girl with silver locks who disrupted and violated the native habitat of bears. So in response to each group, you began to tell the story from the vantage point of the particular character with which each interest group identified: first from the viewpoint of Silver-Locks, focusing on her sprightly nature, her curiosity, and her charm. You would paint her actions as carefree child's play, awakening pity and anxiety in your listeners as you recounted her innocence and fear at being awakened by three roaring bears. Once you told it from the point of view of the largest bear, expressing his anger at having his attempts to provide food for his family thwarted and explaining his desire to eat the little girl as normal and natural animal behavior. And on one occasion you even told it from the smallest bear's point of view, explaining his need for a young friend and how he felt that his parents never understood what it was like being a little bear living in a dense forest without playmates. In each of these cases you used the third person, but you limited yourself to the point of view of a specific person or animal in the story. This would be third person limited.

Distinguishing between points of view might be understood as moving from the most natural form of storytelling to a more complex and sophisticated form of storytelling. Choose the point of view you plan to use by determining just how you yourself relate to the events of the story you are telling and just how sophisticated a writing project you want to attempt.

Level One—First person limited. Have you personally experienced the story? If you have, then you will probably want to write it as you experienced it, first-person point of view limited. First person limited works best when you are writing about your own life or family. If you have a journal or diary at your disposal, you might try writing a first-person account based on the internal feelings and judgments of someone who lived in the past. However, if you have not experienced it yourself, it is probably best to use third person.

Level Two—Third person omniscient. If you have not been one of the players in the story, you might consider writing the story in the third person omniscient. Simply report events as they occurred in the third person, adding your own observations and interpretations as you proceed through the story. Most family writers choose simply to report events.

Level Three—Third person limited. If you want to try your hand at a more sophisticated approach, consider telling the story from the point of view of one of the characters in the story. Determine which character in the story you will use; you may decide this largely based on personal interest or the information you have at your disposal or whether or not you have experienced similar events.

One final rule: once you have decided on the point of view that you will use, be very careful not to shift midway in the story from one point of view to another. Consistency in point of view is essential, and shifting points of view is a mark of immature writing.

Finally, there are many subtle variations of these three, and as you develop as a writer, you might want to consult any one of the several books on creative writing now on the market to explore other possibilities.

CHAPTER 5

EDITING AND REVISING

Some Finishing Touches

STEP ONE: EDIT AND REVISE YOUR SENTENCES

There are scores, if not hundreds, of manuals designed to help the beginner develop his skill as a writer of English. After years of dealing with writing students as well as beginning creative writers, I have observed that most problems can be resolved if the student learns how to write a correct English sentence. Then, if a writer understands clearly what an English sentence is and how to avoid basic sentence errors, she is in a position to address the question of style and to learn how to write a sophisticated sentence.

First, the student must understand what a sentence in English is. Unfortunately, many people will still tell the beginning student that a sentence is a complete idea or thought. No one who has exclaimed in surprise "Ouch!"—providing he or she has thought the problem through carefully—would buy the idea that his or her "Ouch!" was any less than a complete idea or thought. Yet we all have sat obediently in English classes and allowed teachers to pontificate that the test of a correct or complete sentence is that it be a complete thought. Such a test is meaningless.

What then is a correct or complete sentence? Quite simply a complete or correct sentence is by definition a group of words that contains a subject and a predicate. One must then quickly add that this subject and predicate cannot be introduced by a subordinating word that links or subsumes that subject and predicate to another sentence. Thus the group of words "I am" is a complete or correct sentence because it contains the subject "I" and the predicate "am." If we were to write "I think because I am," we would link the complete sentence "I am" with a subordinating word to another sentence, reducing what was originally an independent sentence to a dependent sentence (or what is more typically called a *clause*). Of course sentences become a good deal more complicated, but if you can find a subject and a predicate in a group of words, you probably have a complete sentence.

Many beginning writers find their work corrected by teachers of English because they make errors that are basically violations of the complete or correct sentence concept. Spelling and agreement errors would not come under this category, but knowing how to punctuate and capitalize correctly comes much more easily if one understands how to write a correct English sentence. Learning to control the English sentence, then, means first learning how to avoid basic English sentence errors.

Basic Sentence Errors

The *fragment* is a group of words that does not contain both a subject and a predicate. The group of words "The teacher, with spectacles on nose and sharpened red pencil in hand" is not a complete or correct sentence because it does not have a predicate.

The *comma splice* involves two or more sentences that are separated by a comma. "I came, I saw, I conquered" is technically a group of words with two comma splices. Complete sentences must be separated by a terminal punctuation mark such as a period.

The *run-together sentence* occurs when two or more sentences are placed together with no mark of separation. "The teacher took his red pencil in hand the student looked away in horror." There must be a mark of separation between the words "hand" and "the" such as a period and capital letter or a comma and a word such as "and."

Sophisticated Sentence Errors

Agreement means making certain that the verb is plural or singular in form according to the true subject. Most problems occur when there are phrases or words between the subject and the verb such as in the sentence "One of the students is wrong." Many would use "are" because of the word "students"; however, the true subject is "one" not "students."

Parallelism demands that you use similar grammatical constructions in sequence. "When I was a small child, I loved nothing more than running, jumping, and to pit myself against my friends." The sentence should read "run*ning*, jum*ping*, and pit*ting* myself ...."

Punctuation, though important, is simply too broad a matter for this book. *The Chicago Manual of Style* is the definitive authority and far too detailed for most writers; however, Kate L. Turabian's *A Manual for Writers* is based on the Chicago manual and covers most punctuation rules that writers need to know.

Shift refers to inappropriate changes in person, tense, voice, or key words.

- *Person:* "William came to a point in life when you would think about giving up." Since "William" is in the third person, we cannot use "you." We must continue with the third person: "William came to a point in life when one would think about giving up."

- *Tense:* "I place the paper on the desk, pick up my pen, and began to write." "Began" is past tense; the sentence should read "begin to write."

- *Voice:* "William's son was a real boon during William's time in prison; in short, William was supported throughout those difficult years by a loving family." The first part of this sentence is in the active voice, the second in the passive. Change the second part to read " ...; in short, a loving family supported William throughout those difficult years."

- *Key Words:* "When I was a kid, my primary goal was to become wealthy; now my outstanding goal is to be happy." Moving from "primary" to "outstanding" is a confusing shift.

When it comes to *spelling*, each writer seems to have his or her blind spot. Make a list of words that you commonly misspell such as "accommodate," "effect," "fascinate," "occasion," "occurred," "proceed," "quiet," and "separation." Above all, if you are using a computer, take advantage of your spell-check option. There is almost no reason today for a misspelled word. And do not use contractions; they are not formal usage.

Avoiding Errors in Diction

Diction mainly involves learning how to use words correctly and is the one area on which a beginning writer should focus so that he can avoid words and constructions that mark his work as immature and unsophisticated.

- Distinguish carefully between words such as "affect" and "effect," "accept and "except," "all ready" and "already," "all together" and "altogether," "allusion" and "illusion," "appraise" and "apprise," "emigrant" and "immigrant," "farther" and "further," "imply" and "infer," "oral" and "verbal," and "raise" and "rise."

- Eliminate words and expressions from your writing that do not exist or are considered substandard such as "accidently," "busted," "enthused," "incidently," "irregardless," "should of," and "would of."

- Learn how to spell words that are sounded alike but have distinct and different meanings: "your" for "you're," "capital" for "capitol," "council" for "counsel," "principle" for "principal," "stationary" for "stationery."

- Correctly use words that are commonly misused in everyday English such as "aggravate," "apt," "disinterested," "liable," "likely," "oral," and "verbal."

- *Wordiness* is a difficult concept to teach and probably only comes after years of learning to rewrite. Just remember that writers "oversay" almost everything, and always consider ways to express yourself more directly or simply.

Now as you reconsider what you have written, you might try reading sentences out of order so that you can break the developing logic of the paragraph and focus more directly on whether or not the sentence is complete, that is, contains both a subject and a predicate. Then you might consider more sophisticated matters of style such as parallelism, diction, and wordiness. Finally, most word-processing programs now have grammar checkers which often alert the writer to errors and possible problems. Use them wisely, not slavishly. They raise issues that are often not issues, but they do help.

STEP TWO: USE THE COMPUTER EFFECTIVELY

The computer has made the impossible possible, and the future assures us of even more exciting changes that will render what we marvel at today part of a distant dark age. Still, it amazes me how so many people who use these wonderful technological advances, primarily word-processing and page-layout applications, do not make full use of the features at their fingertips. I have included the following suggestions to facilitate editing and revising on a computer; however, I have assumed that the reader is familiar with both word-processing and page-layout applications. If this is not the case, the suggestions below will not make much sense.

Developing an Outline and Writing the Rough Draft

CLUSTERING

A cluster or tree diagram is one way of developing a rough outline, as mentioned in chapter 2. A writer can simulate this method of outlining in a page-layout application but not in a word-processing application. One types a series of text blocks, each block containing a different concept or idea, and then connects text blocks together with the application's line tool, moving text blocks from point to point as one deems logical. One can argue that using a page-layout program for clustering is more work than it is worth and that clustering is far easier if the writer simply jots ideas down on a page. The real advantage of the computer is that the writer can either expand each text block with details or can copy and paste a text block to another file, or to another point in the same file.

LISTING AND SORTING

Listing is an easy way to generate a rough outline. Given a topic or subject, the writer simply lists ideas as they occur. What makes word-processing applications unique is that they allow the writer to sort lists. However, the writer must first code each item in the list with a number, letter, or symbol before sorting the items in the list.

OUTLINING

Word-processing applications allow the writer, after generating a list of related ideas, to regroup or rearrange those ideas into a working outline. After rearranging ideas into groups or into some kind of logical flow and eliminating ideas that do not fit into the outline, the writer places ideas under other ideas in a secondary position. The process is intuitive and logical, much as if the writer were developing an outline on a piece of paper.

SAVE AND SAVE-AS FEATURES

After completing the outline, the writer saves the file, incorporating the term "outline" somewhere in the file name. Then the writer creates a copy of the original outline through the Save- as feature; in other words, one creates a second file from the "outline" file. However, the writer now gives the "saved-as" file—which is still at this point an outline—the title of the narrative or exposition. If one is a methodical planner and writer, one "fleshes out" the details in the second or "saved-as" file, creating from the outline the story or exposition, the final written product. Still working in the outline mode, the writer can hide text after fleshing out an item in the outline so that one can mentally recapture the flow of the outline. And, of course, the writer can then easily delete those portions of the outline no longer needed.

SIMULTANEOUS WINDOWS

Word-processing applications allow the writer to move easily between portions of the same file or between separate files through the simultaneous window feature. In this way, the writer can consider exactly what one said at another point in the story or exposition, changing either part at will. Scrolling back and forth between sections of a document is not as helpful as examining both sections side by side.

NARROW AND WIDE COLUMNS

Narrow and wide columns also allow the writer similar flexibility, but this feature works best in a page-layout application. Word-processing applications are generally too cumbersome to make this feature much of an advantage. I have seen students place an outline or a kernel idea in a narrow column and expand it in a wide column. Also, the writer can place a graphic on a page, size it down, and develop a narrative or exposition about it in a wide text block.

Locating, Changing, And Relocating Sections

FINDING

The important thing to remember about any find command is that you type in exactly what you want the computer to find. Simple as this may sound, many writers forget that an extra space or return which is normally invisible to the eye can make all the difference in the world to a find command. Normally, you can find whatever you want to find, a word standing by itself or a part of something else; and you can also find according to whether the item is uppercase or lowercase.

INDEXING

Indexing is something that a writer would use to compile an index of words or persons for a piece of writing. You have to code words or sentences yourself; only when you have coded items will the computer generate an index or a listing of items by page number. It is not an editing-find feature.

CHANGING

This feature allows you to change what you have found to something else. It is easy to use, but writers as often as not forget to tell the computer exactly what they want the computer to find or how to change what the computer does find. And there are often codes or ways of indicating changes that the writer can easily forget.

COPYING AND PASTING

Once you have located a word or an item, you can copy the selection and place or paste the copy anywhere you want in the same file or even in another file.

CUTTING AND PASTING

This feature is extremely helpful when you want to relocate a word or a sentence or an entire piece of writing anywhere in the same file or even in another file. In fact, it is the one feature of most word-processing and page-layout applications that gives the writer a sense of godlike control. It is really what makes editing with a computer what it is.

Enhancing Your Writing Visually

FONTS

Generally graphic artists categorize fonts into four typefaces: text, display, decorative, and specialty. *Text* fonts are largely serif faces: Times, Bookman, Bodoni, and Palatino are some examples. There is some overlap with text fonts and *display* or *sans serif* fonts. Helvetica, a sans serif font, is the most popular display font in the world and is even sometimes used as a text font. *Decorative* or *script* and *cursive* fonts (Zaph Chancery is the most common type) are used for invitations or advertisements. Finally, there are *specialty* or *novelty* fonts: Zaph Dingbats is perhaps the best-known example.

One of the first rules of using fonts is to limit the number of typefaces used in a work, generally no more than two or three per page. The question, though, that the writer needs answered is what might be considered the best typefaces. One author (Erfert Fenton, *The Macintosh Font Book*) lists the top ten as Bodoni, Futura, Galliard, Garamond, Goudy Old Style,

Janson, New Baskerville, Optima, Trump Mediaeval, and Univers. You might consider reading what specialists have to say about typefaces before making your final decision.

GRAPHICS

Word-processing applications allow you to import graphics, but anyone who has worked with this feature in a word-processing application would just as well forgo the feature. The only way to work in graphics is to use a page-layout application. A page-layout application used in conjunction with a sophisticated draw application can result in a document that is hard to beat professionally.

CHECKING THE LAYOUT

If you want to know exactly what your document will look like before you print it, you can use features such as Print Preview. This allows you to check for relative positions of text and to avoid too many white spaces and awkward lapses. Of course, the best way to do this is with a page-layout application where you can easily adjust the position and size of text blocks as well as the size and placement of graphics.

Once you preview your text, you can decide if you need to split blocks of text, left or right justify text, and allow for or eliminate white spaces. Remember that one-third to one-half of the text page should be white. Once again, all this can be accomplished if you use a word-processing application, but it is much easier if you use a page-layout application.

STYLE SHEETS

One of the most important features of both word-processing applications and page-layout applications is the style sheet. Each application has a slightly different way to create a style sheet. No matter which application you use, however, you can create consistent typography and format from chapter to chapter or story to story. This saves you countless hours of careful editing and the worry of having to reinvent the wheel each time you sit down to write.

Correcting Errors

SPELLING CORRECTION

Word-processing applications generally provide a fail-safe way to avoid spelling errors. Obviously, the writer has to watch for homonyms (words with the same pronunciation but with different meanings), and the computer will not alert you to a word that is spelled correctly but used incorrectly.

THESAURUS AND DICTIONARY

These features allow quick access to words or meanings. They are helpful and keep you from the troublesome task of having to look up words in a book.

GRAMMAR OR STYLE CHECKERS

There are several grammar or style checkers, and most leave much to be desired. Still, they can be helpful; even at their worst, they force you to answer questions about what you have written.

Giving Proper Credit

There are three ways to reference material in a document: parenthetical references, endnotes, and footnotes. Obviously parenthetical references and endnotes are not a problem, but those of us who wrote papers before the advent of computers can remember the all-night typing vigils because we forgot one footnote or had to add another one. And that was in the day when professors checked out our footnotes in the library. All word-processing applications have easy ways to add and delete footnotes at the mere touch of a key; and of course, anyone can easily print out a new copy of a paper with the footnote correction.

ARE YOU READY TO WRITE?

A family history?

To publish a book that will stand as a permanent legacy of your life
and the lives of your family and ancestors?

If for years you've thought and thought about writing a family history but have never been able to get started, or even if you've already started your family history and now need just a little help to complete the task, this may be the opportunity you've been waiting for.

You'll study with Dr. Larry Gouldrup, author of *Writing the Family Narrative* and *Writing the Family Narrative Workbook*

As a student, you will correspond and work directly with Dr. Gouldrup as you organize and write your manuscript. He will review your work and give you specific pointers on how to make your writing more effective and better represent the lives you are portraying. As you complete your manuscript, take advantage of the steps and writing techniques Dr. Gouldrup has developed over years of teaching writing and family history.

- -

Yes, I'm Ready.

I want to write my family history. Please send me information about how I can get started.

Name:_____

Address: _____

City, State, Zip: _____

Mail this coupon today to:
Dr. Larry Gouldrup
26861 Trabuco Road, Box 149
Mission Viejo, CA 92691